The Fire on Fairmont

Reflections on the Impact of One Small Group in Kingdom Building

Audrey Jackson Johnson

Foreword by Reverend Dwight Webster

The Fire on Fairmont: Reflections on the Impact of Small Groups in Kingdom Building

ISBN 1-891773-534

Cover and interior design by Karen Riley Simmons, Word for Word Publications, New Orleans, Design Copyright © 2004 by Karen Riley Simmons

Published by Orman Press, Inc., 4200 Sandy Lake Drive, Lithonia, Georgia 30038

Manufactured and printed in the United States of America.

To the memory of my grandmother, Mary D. Dent Jackson:
She taught me how to "faith" God in all situations and how to love His people;

To my friend, my husband, my lover, my supporter, and my encourager, Deacon Felix Joseph Johnson, Jr.;

To my mother, Dorothy Hudson Jones:
Thank you for your prayers and your love;

To my children, Felix III, Troy, David, Ernest, Mary, and William:
Thank you for being there when I needed you the most;

To my brother, Solomon Jackson, Jr.:
Thank you for your love and support;

To all of those men and women who at one time or another attended the Fairmont Drive Bible Study:
I thank you for being a part of the journey.

Contents

Foreword

"The Baptist Church doesn't teach."

This statement is rife with irony. To some extent, it was the impetus for a marvelous para-church ministry launched in 1976 in the home of a Baptist deacon, Felix Johnson, and his not-yet-answered-her-call-to-preach nurse/educator wife, Audrey Jackson Johnson. The statement is also contrary to the reality of some churches with a Sunday School, Baptist Training Union (BTU), or Christian Education department. The trend toward having a Bible Study with an agenda or curriculum set from outside of the local congregation was just taking hold in the 1970s. But there was something distinctive, something unique about this Bible Study.

Three remarkable things characterized the Bible Study that took place in the quiet Gentilly section of New Orleans. First, despite the suspicions and disbelief of local clerics to the contrary, the Bible Study was never intended, nor did it lead to the eventual formation of a church. Many a home Bible Study or Prayer Meeting has evolved into a church for various and sundry reasons—but not this one. Second, this cooperative venture was a family ministry where the children played a vital role, the wife was a teacher-trainer, and the husband was the priest of the home. Third, "The Fairmont Drive Theological Seminary"— one name among several it has been called—produced converts, witnesses, and preachers, some of whom have become pastors both near and far. Seminary students translated and taught receptive hearers of the Word the best of what they themselves had learned at the New Orleans Baptist Theological Seminary. No, this was not your average, ordinary, run-of-the-mill home Bible Study.

As a grateful pastor who did not have to compete with this historic, highly successful, decade-long endeavor, I urged Rev. Johnson, whom I had the pleasure of licensing and ordaining at the same time as her son, Rev. Troy T. Johnson, to write about her story and her experience some time after the family decided it was time to discontinue the adventure. It was clear to me that the Bible Study helped to bridge the gap between church folk and seminarians, clergy and laity, men and women. *The Fire on Fairmont* promises to be required reading for anyone, local or otherwise, who is serious about Black Church history made here in New Orleans, Louisiana.

Rev. Dwight Webster
Senior Pastor
Christian Unity Baptist Church
New Orleans, Louisiana

Preface

I thank God for my wife, Audrey, and I thank Him for the call that He placed on her life. The Bible Study that she led in our home was a blessing to our family. As priest of our home, I knew that many of the young men who came to the Bible Study looked to see what I did and hear what I said. Audrey and I never had conflicts. I never had to prove who I was. I knew who I was, and I knew that the Lord had chosen her for a special purpose.

The first time her calling became real to me was in 1973 when she was sick. I prayed to the Lord to heal her. The doctors eventually told me that she would be all right, but one of them said she would be crippled. I kept praying. One night, the Lord said, "She'll be all right. I'm going to use her, and you stick by her."

The Lord healed Audrey and put her back on her feet. One day, a while later, I saw a brightness on her face that I had never seen before. That day, she told me that the Lord had called her to preach. I told her that I knew it before she opened her mouth. She asked me why I didn't tell her, and I told her that the Lord didn't tell me to.

It was tough at times hearing men talk about Audrey attending seminary, leading Bible Study, and being called to preach. I heard them talk about her from the pulpit, in the pews, and even in the barbershop. One time, when I was in the barbershop, a man started talking about my wife and her calling to preach. The barber looked at me strangely, thinking, I suppose, that I would say something; but, I didn't. After the man quit talking, another man said, "That's Audrey's husband right there." The man got up and walked out. If I had acted on what people said, Audrey and I would have had arguments all the time.

The Bible Study grew faster and bigger than I thought it would. Sometimes, when I came home from work on Tuesday evenings, I couldn't get in my house. I had to sit on the steps. People came early so they could get a good spot on the floor. I seldom invited anyone. I met Rev. Jim Wynne on the playground one day when

I was out with my sons. A couple of weeks later, I saw him sitting in the Bible Study. To this day, I never asked who invited him. Students brought their girlfriends, boyfriends, husbands, and wives. One woman trailed her husband to see where he was going on Tuesday nights. It ended up that she knew us, and she started attending every week. My doctor, my pharmacist, and even some of the folks who worked with me attended. In fact, the Bible Study branched off for a while, and Audrey taught a class at lunchtime on my job at Shell Oil Company.

The blessing was that folks were saved. They got to know the Lord, they brought others, and they took what they learned back to their homes and churches and taught others. In time, preachers around the city began to understand the purpose of the Bible Study; and in time, many of them began to accept and appreciate the work that God had laid upon the hands and heart of my wife, Audrey Jackson Johnson.

Felix J. Johnson, Jr.

Acknowledgements

My first thanks is to God the Father; Jesus Christ, my Savior and Lord; and to the precious Holy Spirit for guidance and giving me memory of these past events. I thank you, for by your grace this project was started and completed. I am thankful for my father in the ministry, my pastor, Reverend Dwight Webster, Senior Pastor of Christian Unity Baptist Church, New Orleans, who encouraged me to complete this work. He saw in me what I did not see in myself—an up-and-coming writer.

I recognize that no work is a successful effort without the support and assistance of others; the Lord sent people who offered their skills and coaching for this first-time writer. I thank God for Freddi Williams Evans who encouraged me every step of the way—reading, editing, and making suggestions as I began to put pen to paper. She was patient with me as I struggled to recall events; and her enthusiasm motivated me to push harder to reach the deadlines. I thank God for Karen Celestan, a certified editor, for transcribing tapes, editing and offering her suggestions. I am also grateful to God for Jarvis DeBerry, a columnist, writer, and poet, for his editing and suggestions. I thank God for Rev. Dr. Kirk Byron Jones, Kelsey-Owens Professor, Andover Newton Theological School in Massachusetts, for his leadership in helping some of us who were members of the Bible Study to share our reflections about the study. I thank him for his knowledge and guidance in helping us to get started.

I am indebted to Vanessa Polk for her arduous labor as a typist and editor. I am grateful for the many readers of the manuscript: Rev. Dwight Webster, Rev. Dr. Kirk Byron Jones, Mary Washington, Karen Riley Simmons, Eve Francois, Ashleigh Gilbert, Rev. Edward Morris, Rev. Donald Boutté, Rev. Mattie Stone Williams, Gwendolyn Tate-Smith, Rev. Troy Johnson, and Vera Warren-Williams.

I am thankful for my Christian Unity family. I am grateful for your prayers and words of encouragement.

Introduction

This book is about a home Bible Study that began in 1976 and lasted for over 10 years. I am Audrey Jackson Johnson, and the Bible Study took place at 3825 Fairmont Drive, the home I share with my husband Felix and our sons Felix III, Troy, and David. This work gives reflections on how the "fire" of the Bible Study started. It is not meant to be a how-to book. It is a what-happened book. It is a book that shows proof of the power of small groups; and it attempts to share what impact the Bible Study had upon the lives of those who attended.

My prayer is that those who read *The Fire on Fairmont* will see the power of God preparing my family for our purpose at that period of our Christian growth. I also pray that readers recognize the influence this small group had and continues to have on community and church leaders. I am aware that we may never know the full impact of the Bible Study, because it was not a research project, but a journey controlled by the Holy Spirit.

Many have encouraged me to tell this story about the Fairmont Drive Bible Study; however, the most ardent voice was that of my pastor, Rev. Dwight Webster of the Christian Unity Baptist Church in New Orleans. His relentless questions fueled my efforts: How did we get started? How did God get my attention to begin this ministry in our home? How could I hear God in a city that is known for its culture, its music, its food, entertainment, and worldly atmosphere?

New Orleans is known nationally and internationally for Mardi Gras and the Mardi Gras Indians, and for its festivals—the Jazz & Heritage Festival, the Essence Music Festival, the French Quarter Festival, the Tomato Festival, and others. New Orleans is famous for its food—gumbo, jambalaya, shrimp Creole, pralines, red beans and rice, and much more. We are known for our tourism industry. This city is one of the few places in the country where there is entertainment available 24 hours a day. People come here to have a good time; the lights are always on.

New Orleans is home to an array of rich cultural influences—French, Spanish, African, and others. There are Creole-speaking people, Cajuns, Asians, and Latinos. We are recognized for celebrating our cultural diversity. We are known for Voodoo, Marie Laveau and the Seven Sisters, and for second-line parades on Sundays, at funerals and at other events. New Orleans also boasts two private, historically Black Universities, Dillard University and Xavier University, as well as a state-run Black University, Southern University at New Orleans (SUNO).

The city is also known for its many barrooms, taverns, nightclubs, casinos, men's clubs, and entertainment houses. In New Orleans, a person can get a drink at any hour of the night—or of the day, for that matter. New Orleans has rightly earned her title: "The City That Care Forgot." But, thanks be to God, He did not forget this city. In spite of what was going on around me in this metropolis, the Lord got my attention to start a Bible Study.

How did He get me to turn aside? From what bush of

flaming fire did He speak to me? The Lord used our niece, Lisa Green Derry. As a young Christian, she wanted to learn more about the Bible, and repeatedly asked me about starting a class. It soon became apparent that the voice I was hearing was not just Lisa's, but I was hearing from God through her.

During the 1970s, there were not many weekly Bible classes in our churches. That lack created a void in our community. The Scriptures possess practical applications above and beyond the obvious that should be evident in our everyday living and community involvement. It was and continues to be important for the Black church to address the Christian walk in the racist environment of our society and country.

The Black church has always been the strong foundation in our community. Leadership and economic development, social issues and social awareness traditionally have been major parts of its agenda. The training we have received as members in the church has been designed to teach us how to survive as a people and as a community.

The church was always composed of the people in the community—families (immediate and extended family members), educators, business people, caretakers of the sick and those in need, laborers, elders, and many other professionals.

In this book, I revisit the role that the church has played in my life and the influence it had on my community. The greatest challenge for me as I wrote was to share, especially with youth and young adults, the history and role of the Black church as well as the significance of small study groups. It was my desire that they capture the impact small groups could have on a larger group in ministry.

People from across the Greater New Orleans Metropolitan area were drawn to the Bible Study. Its mission and impact crossed religious affiliations, educational backgrounds, economic and social levels, age, gender, and even the Mississippi River. The flaming presence of the Holy Spirit settled upon our home, and many came to experience what God was doing. Thousands of prayers were prayed, hundreds of lessons were taught, and many lives were changed. Tucked within the pages of this book are some of their reflections and testimonies.

It is my prayer that this book will strengthen your resolve to have a closer walk with God, encourage you to be obedient to the voice of the Master and to do His will, and inspire you to pick up where I left off. Written from my perspective as a Baptist and a woman preacher, this is my story.

Keep the Fire burning!

The Fire on Fairmont

Reflections on the Impact of One Small Group in Kingdom Building

A Burning Desire
Preparation for My Journey

Before I formed you in your mother's womb I knew you; before you were born I sanctified you. —Jeremiah 1:5

The Lord chooses us for His purpose and gives us gifts and talents to fulfill that purpose. Sometimes to understand what God is doing and has done, we must practice Sankofa, a West African term often expressed by the late Dr. Morris F. X. Jeff, Jr., a prominent leader in the New Orleans community. As summarized on his funeral program, Sankofa requires you to "Retrieve your past, live it in the present, for the future." In essence, I can't go forward until I look back at my past to embrace all of its riches.

I was born in New Orleans' Charity Hospital on October 7, 1936, to Dorothy and the late Solomon Jackson, Sr. I lived with my parents until their separation, and my father brought my brother, Solomon, and me to his mother, Mary D. Jackson. Solomon was about five years old, and I was six when our grandmother, a strong Christian woman who had it all together, took us in. Solomon and I were not from a "broken home" as mainstream America would like to have categorized us. When our grandmother began to take care of us, she was already a senior citizen and a widow, but "Mama," as we called her, provided the best home and the most secure environment that any child could ever want.

Mama was active in the Stranger Home Baptist Church and was called a missionary because she was known in the community and surrounding areas for her jubilee singing. She loved the Lord and the church, and had us there every time the doors opened. We attended choir rehearsal, though we were not choir members, Prayer Service, Sunday School, Baptist Training Union (BTU), and Speaking Meeting, a period for testimonies on the Thursday or Friday evening, and sometimes the Sunday morning, before the communion observance.

A Burning Desire—Preparation for My Journey

As a result of my childhood religious experiences, I learned early about the church's relationship to the community, for the church was composed of the community. When someone in the community was sick, whether churched or un-churched, the church mothers and deacons took care of him. The pastor, highly respected in the community, lived among the people. Teachers, dentists, doctors, pharmacists, and principals who were a part of our church lived in our community. Those icons motivated my peers and me to reach for high goals and get a good education. Even today, I have not forgotten that sense of community or how much it has influenced my life.

Because of her love and wisdom, Mama had the greatest impact on my life. When you are reared by wise seniors, you often think very differently from most of your peers. Mama used to say, "You've got old folks' sense."

Our home was always open to family and friends, and sometimes strangers. We lived in what was called a "shotgun" house at 2616 South Prieur Street in the "back o' town" area of New Orleans. Its three rooms consisted of a front room, a middle room, and a kitchen. The toilet was on an outside porch. We were taught to keep our house clean—inside and outside. Meals were cooked on a pot-bellied stove and eaten on a wooden table covered with oilcloth. Mama, an excellent cook, loved to have company. Sometimes during the holidays, we would have relatives come from all over the country. Staying at local hotels was not an option, so 10 or 12 people slept at the house. The kitchen was turned into a two-bed sleeping area, and we had great fellowship and fun.

Mama talked about the Lord and His goodness all the time. She testified of His grace and mercy, expressed how much she loved Him, and imparted this knowledge and wisdom to Solomon and me. At an early age, we accepted Christ and were baptized together at Stranger Home Baptist Church by the late Rev. Eugene Powell. Our church, Stranger Home, did not have a baptismal pool, so about 10 candidates marched approximately four blocks from our church at South Miro and Third Streets for baptism at the Mount Era Baptist Church at South Prieur and Third Streets.

We wore all-white candidate "outfits"—the girls with their heads tied in white cloth and the boys in their all-white outfits with white armbands. These uniforms were very "Baptist." We sang as we made our way to the pool. I can almost hear the voices, "Let us go down to Jordan and be baptized." I was unafraid of the water; I came up happy. After the ceremony, the girls put on white dresses with veils on their head, and the boys donned all-white suits and shirts. Each new convert had to wear white shoes. This attire was a tradition borrowed from the Catholic Church.

We were taught how to live as Christians by precept and example. This teaching and sense of community provided what I needed to grow and face a world that was hostile to Black females. Later, as a teenager, I followed my aunt Rosilie Stewart and became a member of the Ebenezer Baptist Church, under the leadership of Rev. Dr. L. E. Landrum. Aunt Rosilie and her sister, my aunt Rohilda Spencer, were also role models for me. Aunt Rohilda was a member of Stronger Hope Baptist Church; the late Rev. J. Carter was the pastor. My two aunts were known as two of the great gospel soloists in the Crescent City. At that time in my life, I had begun to sing more and more and was subsequently exposed to such great gospel artists as Mahalia Jackson, the Alex Bradford Singers, the Jackson Gospel Singers, Bessie Griffin, Helen Stevens, and others around the country.

Ebenezer Baptist Church sparked my spiritual growth. I learned to speak before the congregation and became even more involved in the singing ministry. Many of the older congregants would say, "Girl, you've got a calling on your life."

I had no idea what they were talking about. I was busy enjoying the church. It was a safe haven, and it provided opportunities for my friends and me to "hang out" after school. We completed our homework at church. The pastor bought us food and encouraged us to do well in school. The church even assisted me financially to meet my high school graduation budget.

Sometime later, a member of that church, Sister Mary Landrum, placed my name in a pool for testing for a college scholarship to Southern University in Baton Rouge. I got the scholarship and in four years graduated from Southern with a B.A. in Psychology. Originally, I had entered Southern to begin a program in nursing, which was my passion. However, the university failed to get the program up and running. In fact, the program was discontinued, and I changed my major to psychology.

My friends and roommates on campus used to call me "Miss Florence Nightingale" or "The Preacher." I was not aware that I was showing those characteristics. I knew of my love for the Lord and my deep desire to know more about His Word. Most of the churches at that time had a Sunday School, but no weekly Bible Study classes. When I graduated from Southern and returned home to New Orleans in 1959, I had been married for approximately two years to my wonderful friend, Felix Johnson, Jr.

I met Felix through a girlfriend, the late Shirley

Gage, when I was a senior at McDonogh 35 Senior High School. He took me to my high school class night on our first date. Clean-cut and well dressed, he was a gentleman with a great sense of humor, and he treated me like a lady. He was passionate about his faith and a good listener. In time, a true sense of friendship developed, and I learned more about him and his personal relationship with Christ. On some Sundays, Felix visited me at Ebenezer Baptist Church, and eventually won my grandmother's heart. Of all the boyfriends I had, she liked him most. Actually, Mama loved Felix.

When I went to Southern University, Felix was drafted into the Army, and our courtship continued through the mail. At that time, we had known each other about a year. After six months in the Army, he had an opportunity to be discharged, and he took advantage of it. Felix's faith played a major role in us getting married. Mama had always told me to marry a man who was "in the church." Felix was the kind of man I was looking to share my life with. The way he practiced his faith and related to people were examples of what Mama had advised me to consider when choosing a husband. He treated me with respect and loving tenderness. We were married September 7, 1957, in a quiet family wedding at Ebenezer Baptist Church followed by a small reception at my grandmother's house.

When I was a student at Southern, I decided to go only to Vespers, the mandatory evening worship services on campus, rather than to go off campus to church on Sunday mornings. If I took the bus off campus to church, by the time the bus returned, the line in the cafeteria would extend outside the doors and around the corner. I would have to stand in the sun and sometimes rain in my Sunday-go-to-meeting clothes—stockings, heels and hat. Many times, when I got inside, the food would have run out. Not only was that the last meal the cafeteria served on Sundays, I did not have money to buy food from the "canteen" and, as a female student, I was not allowed to leave campus to get food or for any reason. Consequently, my church routine was so interrupted that, by the time I returned home, I had lost interest in regular church attendance and lacked commitment to the body of Christ.

When I stopped attending church regularly Felix continued to go to all of the services, including Baptist Training Union (BTU). He was patient with me and never insisted that I go to church. He would come back and tell me how good service was, who asked about me, and who said they missed me. I felt guilty, but I would not say so. In retrospect, I am sure that was his way of motivating me to return to church. He loved church so much that he was known as a church man and a preacher's friend by his friends.

Because Felix was so committed to the Lord, the impact of his faith drew me back to regular church attendance. Reared in a Christian home, his parents, Felix J. Johnson, Sr. and the late Vivian Glenn Johnson, loved the church; and so did their son. He is a strong and compassionate man; I have been extremely blessed to have him as my husband, friend, and father of my children.

Why am I sharing our story? Because I want you

to capture the vision of God's preparation for the work that He had for my family to do. The sum total of our life experiences served as a foundation for all that God would do in us and through us. While we could not see it then, every circumstance prepared us to discover and be obedient to the purpose and plans God had for us.

In 1959, I became pregnant. Felix and I were so excited! We looked forward with great anticipation to the birth of our baby. However, our excitement was short-lived. In my fifth month, I went into labor and the child was stillborn. It was devastating to both of us. Feeling lost with no plan or sense of direction, I couldn't see—until much later—how God would use our pain to prepare us for the mission ahead.

When I was in the hospital, I received very poor care from the staff and some of the doctors. I remember one doctor who had to change my IV from one hand to another, said to me, "Nigger, you know you're gonna die anyway."

When they had delivered the fetus, I remember that

same doctor saying, "Uh, this thing is ugly!"

Even some of the Black women who were on the nursing staff talked to me and other Black patients in a dehumanizing manner. Felix was not allowed to visit or call me while I was hospitalized, in keeping with the hospital's policies at that time. When I got home and told him what happened, he wept.

As a result of going through that ordeal in the hospital, I made up my mind to return to the field of nursing and become an excellent nurse. I enrolled in Dillard University and graduated three years later, in 1963, with a Bachelor of Science degree in Nursing (B.S.N.). Several months later, I passed the boards and became a Registered Nurse. My first job as an RN was with the United States Public Health Service Hospital (USPH) where I was a supervisor of Obstetrics and Gynecology (OBGYN) and Newborn Nursery.

In 1964, I had a successful pregnancy and delivery of an eight-pound boy, Felix, III. Our seventh year anniversary was September 7, 1964. Lil' Felix, as we called him, was born September 8, 1964. What a joyous occasion! After two heartbreaking experiences, God had blessed us with a healthy baby. Lil' Felix grew up to be a wise child with a strong spirit of discernment. Known for his profound sense of humor, he was also a very caring and compassionate person. These attributes remain very much a part of who Lil' Felix is today. He is much like his father.

In 1966, God blessed us with another son. Troy was eight pounds, five ounces. Born 19 months after Lil' Felix, Troy brought additional joy and satisfaction. He grew up to be very gregarious. He made friends quickly and never met a stranger. He was confronting and adventurous. Very little has changed about him today. I am often told that Troy is very much like me.

Five years later, God gave us David. He was born in 1971 at eight pounds, two ounces. His two older brothers gave him so much love. He was known in the family as the lover. David loved his family and depended a lot on his brothers for support. He has characteristics of both his father and me—a strong mind and a tender heart. All three sons were born at USPH.

In 1972, our son Felix, III, met a friend, Ernest Franklin, in elementary school. Felix talked to him about the Lord and encouraged his classmate to accept Jesus as his Savior. After meeting Ernest's mother, Felix invited him to church. Ernest was later baptized and grew up with our sons. We became Ernest's extended family, and as our "son," he lived in our home with his "brothers." He called us Pops and Mom. Ernest brought to this family much love. He grew up to be the son with a mind for entrepreneurship. He had a genuine love for family—both his blood family members and for us, his extended family.

I joined my husband's church, the Gloryland Mount Gillion Baptist Church pastored by the Rev. Herbert L. Johnson, in 1959. I made this decision in order to be with my husband as we grew in the Lord and in our relationship as family. Rev. Johnson's preaching helped me to understand even more the need for the study of the Word. He was a good preacher, and I had not been exposed to that kind of preaching before. Felix and I were very active in all facets of the church. We were both in Sunday School, Baptist Training Union (BTU), and sang in the choir, of which Felix was president. I served as director of the Youth Department and was one of the announcing clerks for the church's radio broadcast. In all of this, the Lord was preparing us to be leaders for the Fairmont Drive Bible Study.

After the death of Rev. Johnson, Rev. John Burkett became pastor. During this period, God really began to reveal to me the true mission of His church. When I began to share my ideas about how the church could make a difference in the community and how its mission was to develop leaders and send them out to work in the vineyard, I met opposition immediately. I thought that our church should work with other churches in the community; we should create an after-school program; we should teach Bible Study; and we should feed hungry children. However, it was the 1960s, I was a woman, and that pastor was not ready to hear what I thought.

In 1968, I began working for the Orleans Parish

School Board as an instructor in the Adult Practical Nursing program. In 1973, I had a miscarriage, and major complications kept me in intensive care on a respirator for fourteen days. I had multiple pulmonary emboli (blood clots in lungs) and congestive heart failure. The doctors had said that my prognosis was very poor; but God healed me and raised me up. This was another difficult experience that God used to prepare me for the work ahead of us.

My recovery and convalescence took one year. While I was on sabbatical leave from the Orleans Parish school system, I felt the Lord dealing with me, and I made a decision to go to seminary. This in itself is another story.

At the time, a woman going to seminary was almost unheard of in our community. A whole new world opened up for me. Although I learned a lot of meaningful information, I had never experienced racism and sexism such as I did at the New Orleans Baptist Theological Seminary (NOBTS). With only 25 Black students,—of which approximately eight were women—in a student body of about 400, there was very little support. However, by the grace of God and the support of my husband, I was able to stand my ground and maintain a sense of focus on my twofold purpose: to learn more about the Word of God and prepare leaders who would influence and teach others.

In two years, I completed my seminary studies and graduated with a Master's of Religious Education (M.R.E.). I was still unaware of how the Lord was preparing me to go forth to minister to the whole person. In time, I would understand how psychology would help me to deal with the mind; the nursing degree would help to address the physical needs; and a degree in religion would help me address the spiritual needs. This training and exposure helped me to become a better speaker for Women's Day Programs, celebrations, workshops, and seminars.

While in seminary, I recognized that many of our churches still did not conduct weekly Bible Study classes. Consequently, during the 1970s, many African Americans sought nurture in predominately white, charismatic congregations. I was concerned. Many of the preachers and teachers in those churches were neither culturally sensitive nor culturally competent regarding the African-American experience. Some with whom I shared my thoughts did not think there was cause for concern. However, I knew that the cultural heritage of a people must be addressed in order to make the Word applicable to their lives—just as Jesus, who was fully divine and fully human, acknowledged and practiced his Jewish culture and religious beliefs. The African-American experience with God is unique, and requires that those who teach and lead us be cognizant of the innate dynamics. The need for a Bible Study class became more and more evident, and I was becoming more and more willing to fulfill His purpose in my life.

It Only Takes A Spark

Pursuing Purpose

For we are God's workmanship, created in Christ Jesus to do good works, which God prepared in advance for us to do.
—Ephesians 2:10 (NIV)

To find one's purpose in life is so rewarding. Sometimes God uses people around us to help us identify our purpose. As I stated earlier, God used my niece Lisa to speak to me about beginning the Bible Study. At that time, she was pursuing her bachelor's degree at Xavier University. Lisa was reared Methodist; however, after visiting the Gloryland Mount Gillion Baptist Church, she decided to become Baptist and was baptized by immersion while pregnant with her first child, Dana. During the same time, I was pursuing my master's degree in Religious Education at NOBTS.

Lisa came to me and asked me to begin a Bible Study.

She said, "I want to learn the Bible," and continued to inquire about a starting date. God used her persistence to motivate Felix and me to do what I had been hearing Him speak in my spirit.

God continued to speak to us through Lisa as He took us through this season of preparation. Through all of our experiences He had been preparing us for this work. I would discover that what God was saying to me, He also was saying to my husband. Together we talked with the boys and, as a family, we acknowledged and accepted what God was calling us to do. Yet, I was still a little slow in moving forward to put it into place.

One day, a seminary student whose name I do not recall, came to our house, as many of them often did. Upon entering, he said, "My God, this is a sanctuary. I can feel the presence of the Holy Spirit in this place. I have heard so much about your home. Have you thought about starting a Bible Study for others to come and learn?"

That was the last confirmation I needed. God was leading us to get started and, regardless of the opposition we perceived and anticipated, we were to begin the work immediately; so we did.

The opposition soon became a reality. Many of the local pastors and male preachers spoke negatively about the Bible Study. In the beginning months, Felix witnessed deacons from our church driving by our house on Tuesday nights to check things out. Even though our church did not have a Bible Study class, members of the church were intimidated and reluctant to attend the one at our home. Only a few of the members came to study with us; others were afraid they would get in trouble with the pastor. Regardless of who did or did not attend, we followed the lead of the Holy Spirit.

Felix and I were very clear that the Bible Study was not about starting a church. It was to have an impact on the church. The purpose of the Bible Study was to develop leaders and to give people God's Word the best we knew how. Students could then go back to their churches to do their jobs, and become an inspiration, or an agitator who would stir up the interest of people who had a thirst for the Word of God.

Our family had moved to 3825 Fairmont Drive, our first purchased home, in 1972. The Bible Study caught fire in the fall of 1976. Of all our concerns regarding the study, having people in our home was never one of them. Our home had always been open to visitors, family, friends, and strangers alike. Many times we did not lock our doors. On the few occasions when we did, people wanted to know why. I told Lisa when we would start and that she could invite some friends.

The Fire

The Fire on Fairmont Drive started with the spark of seven or eight students. The plan was to meet once a month on Tuesdays from 7:00 p.m. to 8:00 p.m. on the floor in the empty dining room. The room had one piece of furniture, a piano, and carpet on the floor. As the group grew, we expanded to the living room, and we began to meet weekly with an average of 40 students. We used what little furniture we had—the sofa, two living room chairs, and five kitchen chairs. The chairs and sofa were for the elderly and physically challenged. The floor was for everyone else. Many students rushed to the house to get a comfortable place on the floor where they would sit for approximately an hour. When the Bible Study session ended, we helped each other up and formed the prayer circle amidst grunts, groans and sighs of relief from sitting on the floor.

The Format

When the group first began we had a repast, but because of the expense, we had to reduce the menu to water and drinks—soft drinks, that is. Besides, when we had food, some would linger and talk for hours.

The classes began with devotion: a song, a Scripture, and prayer. Each night, two students were randomly assigned to lead the devotion. Then the teacher began the lesson and taught for an hour. The Bible was the book of choice, and the King James Version was the translation most used. Students received outlines from some of the teachers and were encouraged to keep notes. Instruction was three-dimensional—thinking, feeling, and doing.

Some teachers used overhead projectors, slides, 16mm film projectors, and various other creative methods to ensure that the study produced strong teaching and learning opportunities. The teachers encouraged dialogue and stimulated discussions about how to apply each lesson to the students' lives and daily experiences.

The Foundation

I was the first teacher. I taught an overview of the Gospel of John for about three months. Why the Gospel of John? I had learned from my seminary professors and other pastors that all new Bible students should begin their journey by looking at Jesus the Christ through the eyes of John. We know that Jesus was both human and divine. However, John's Gospel focuses on Jesus' divinity, and that was a good place to begin. We started by using the simple method of having students read a number of verses from the Scripture and then discussing them as a group. Although some students were very poor readers, others encouraged and helped them. This motivated some to return to school to complete their Graduate

Equivalency Degree (G.E.D.). Others returned to college to complete their studies.

Since there was a great need for training in the local church, I became determined for the Bible Study to prepare students to discover and use their gifts to build up the kingdom of God. In the two rooms of our home, we discipled new believers, edified the saints, and witnessed to the lost. We diligently sought God's face for direction on how to lead the Bible Study and who would teach the classes.

As I began to complete the study of John, the Lord led me to get students from the seminary to teach. The instructions that I gave to them were simple: Select a book of the Bible and be prepared to teach it for approximately three months, or longer, if you desire. NOBTS was within walking distance of our home. The student body was primarily White American males. The Black male students were upcoming leaders, but very few pastors and churches embraced them or provided a place for them to practice their gifts. Therefore, 3825 Fairmont Drive was a fertile ground for them to come and teach the Word. It was a win-win situation for everyone. They had an opportunity to use their skills, and the students were being taught as seminarians. There was no threat for them here. They were free to teach the Word. We were not forming a church, so they did not have to worry about positions, polity, or politics.

The first NOBTS student to accept the challenge to teach the class was Rev. Harold Ray of Hattiesburg, Mississippi. Harold lived on campus with his wife, Betty, and worked in addition to going to school. On Tuesday evenings, he would rush from his job to make it to the house in time. He taught the book of Acts. He had taken an exegesis of the book of Acts in seminary, so he decided to teach that same exegesis to the Bible class. During the class, you could almost feel the students listening.

Dialogue that came forth showed the students struggling with questions and trying to resolve what God was saying to them. They enjoyed themselves so much that some suggested we start a church. Again, Felix and I continued to make it clear that we were not starting a church. The Bible Study did not collect offerings and there were no "dos and don'ts" to be a part of the group. All a person had to do was come.

The greatest reward we received was knowing that the students were inviting others. Felix and I did not take ownership of the Bible Study. We seldom recruited others to come. We knew this was not our work; it was the Lord's work. We shared the feeling that God was using this home. He had chosen us to do His work with His people. It was the students who went out and shared what they helped to develop—the Bible Study. They witnessed, recruited, and invited others to become a part of the group.

The Fruit

Many came searching to find the answers to everyday questions and for hope and peace. Some came to grow in the relationship with the God they already knew. Some came looking for support and encouragement. They came, rain or shine. In our home many accepted Jesus

Christ as their personal Savior, many returned to the church, many returned to God, and many were baptized at the church of their choice. Some met and married their soul mates in the fellowship, and some became clear about their calling and their God-given gifts. Because there was an atmosphere of liberty, people came. There were the educated and undereducated, people of various professions—doctors, teachers, and administrators. Some were in the medical field and some were small business owners. There were social workers, hard-working laborers, single parents, grandparents, students, and others.

The Faithful

We never cancelled the Bible Study. Even when we were on vacation, we left the house key in a stove in the garage. Lisa and Donald, another student, were responsible for the key. They opened the house for Bible Study and, when it was over, locked the door and placed the key back in the stove. It was amazing; not one time did we miss anything in our home. No one took anything. Nothing was locked—neither inside doors, nor closets.

God protected us. People came to learn, and learn they did! Felix and I and our children also learned.

Even when one finds his or her purpose and hears God clearly, everything will not always go smoothly and easily. I once heard a preacher say, "You may become tired in the work but not tired of the work." Although I was passionate about the study of God's Word and for sharing it with others, I must admit that there were times when we were physically tired and mentally drained. Nevertheless, God gave us strength. Our commitment to get people to love the Lord and His Word; to learn the Scriptures for themselves and not just depend on what someone else told them; and to lead the students to walk by faith and live a righteous life, compelled us to keep moving forward.

The Bible class met consistently. No holidays, festivals, or special occasions cancelled the study. We met on Mardi Gras night, after students had been out witnessing during the day. The fun and revelry did not stop them. They came seeking, they came thirsty, and they came waiting to hear, to learn, and to grow. The impact upon their lives was so great that 27 years later, many of the students say they still have some of the notes that they took while in class.

The rain did not stop them. The cold did not stop them, nor did the heat. The one big air conditioner window unit we had was not able to completely cool the house when it was extremely hot, as it gets in New Orleans, but they came.

Sparks from the Fire on Fairmont were spreading rapidly. The class was composed of students from various denominations and backgrounds. There were the Baptists, Catholics, Methodists, and those who were members of the Church of God in Christ, Church of God, Holiness, and Non-Denominational churches; the saved and the unsaved; young and old, all who came with a thirst for the Word of God. The students filled every room in the house. There was not a vacant place to rest if needed. The Lord kept things going and no one got sick. We never thought about what would happen if we were ill and had to be on bed rest. The Lord kept us in good health.

The Future

Again, the primary reason for the growth of the Bible Study was that there were few weekly Bible studies in the local churches. So, when students found this one, the Holy Spirit moved them to invite others to study the Word with us. During class one night, the Lord revealed to me some information about the church. I looked around the room and saw the students as never before. The Lord revealed to me that the church has everything she needs for kingdom building and ministry. In that small group of approximately 40, there were mothers, fathers, teachers, nurses, doctors, dentists, pharmacists, small business owners, college students, musicians and other gifted people. He said very clearly again that the church has everything she needs to do the work. We were totally unaware of all of the potential preachers and pastors who were being trained to lead God's people. I thought I knew the power of small groups in the body of Jesus Christ; but God was helping me to see His workings in small groups like never before.

The Small Group

My interest in learning more about small groups grew during my training in Clinical Pastoral Care Education (CPE) to become a chaplain. I took four units of CPE, a yearlong program, at Southern Baptist Hospital in New Orleans. During that time, I wrote a paper entitled "The Small Group and Its Effectiveness in the Local Church." I was aware that many pastors called small groups "cliques," emphasizing the negative. However, I saw many small groups as effective cells working to progress the work of the church. These groups will always be there—the choir, the women's ministry, each Sunday School class, the deacons' ministry, the youth ministry, the children's ministry, the seniors' ministry, and many, many more.

Sometimes while on their way to Bible class, students met people they knew or did not know on the bus, in the grocery store, or on the streets. They would invite them to the study, and many of those persons came. Some accepted Christ and continued to attend the Bible Study regularly. They found their places in the group. Students began to bond and found daily prayer partners. I remember one of the students sharing with me that he did not have a car, but would take the bus from across the river. It was not unusual for someone in the Bible class to take him home.

The Children's Class

Adults brought their babies, toddlers, older children, and adolescents to class with them. Felix and I knew we would have to address the need for teaching the children while they were young. We were being called by the Holy Spirit to train up these children. As the Bible Study grew, we had to begin a new class for the children. We were aware of the need for children to be children, and to meet Jesus at an early age.

Our Own Children

Our own children were a part of that group. We knew that they had an awareness of God and who Jesus was. They attended church regularly, were Sunday School students, and prayed together as a family, but needed to grow in the Lord. Our children never complained to us about the Bible Study. They looked forward to seeing their friends on Tuesday nights. We needed to be careful not to overwhelm them and forget about their own growth and development as well as their need to have a balanced life.

If our children were involved in some outside activity in school or the community, they attended those functions. We did not want to make the Bible Study a burden for them. Our youngest son, David, played football from a young age, and loved it. David did not miss practice or his games, and his daddy was there for all of them. I would make them as often as I could. Our oldest son, Felix, worked after school, but made it home before the class was over. He worked for Kentucky Fried Chicken and many nights brought chicken home for the class. Troy, our second son, was involved in music and teaching the Bible Study. Our children were well rounded.

Felix, my husband, worked for an oil company here in the city and was off by 4:00 or 5:00 p.m. I taught nursing for the Orleans Parish School Board. We both had our careers, but knew what was important. Our family was important to us, and we knew that there was a need for us to keep focused on the Lord's work. As we grew, we learned to balance the jobs, the family, and the Bible Study.

As the classes and fellowship grew in the Lord, the members learned to discern the needs of each other. Many times, the Lord answered our prayers through people in the Bible Study. I recall a time when Felix and I had a financial need, but did not share it with anyone. We asked the Lord to open a way for us to meet our obligation. Within a few days, we found an envelope in our mailbox with our name on it. Inside was money and a note that stated, "The Lord told us to give this to you." We were blessed by that gift.

At Christmas time, the Bible Study focused on helping people who were really in need, offering service as a Christmas present to Jesus. In order to do this we needed to identify whom the needy people were. A physician who was a member of the Bible Study contacted some of his patients and got permission to give us their names. Rather than giving the usual Christmas baskets, the students called and visited them to determine their needs. We found that some needed their electricity turned on, some needed bed covers, some needed clothing, and some needed food. We learned how to contact those with the political clout to get electricity turned on, water service restored, and plumbing repaired. We learned how to be advocates for people.

The students were overwhelmed by their experience and humbled by how God used them to be a blessing in the lives of others. They walked away from those encounters more sensitive toward their responsibility to the community. It only takes one spark to get a fire burning. This spark ignited a desire within the hearts of the students to loose the chains of injustice, set the oppressed free, and provide for the poor and needy. It enlightened our minds and helped us to maintain our focus as we each pursued God's purpose for our individual lives.

Kindling the Fire
Learning from Others

Day after day, in the temple courts and from house to house, they never stopped teaching and proclaiming the good news that Jesus is the Christ. —Acts 5:42

The vision I had for the Bible Study was to instill the Word of God within people, encourage them to stay with their local church body, and prepare them to pass on what they were learning to others. Rev. Kenneth Thompson reminded me in his teaching that a student is not a cup to be filled, but a fire to be kindled. Therefore, I wanted the students' gifts ignited so that they would find their purpose, grow and develop spiritually, and influence others so that they, too, may have the desire to grow in God's grace and knowledge.

The Faith-in-Action Evangelistic Team

The Faith-in-Action Evangelistic Team, led by

Marshall Truehill and Thomas "Chip" Glover, trained us in street witnessing. Faith-in-Action was an evangelism ministry whose primary focus was reaching the lost in the community and educating the body of Christ in effective street witnessing. The team worked in the church, on the street, and in prisons.

Faith-in-Action also accepted students as volunteers to work within the ministry and experience the administrative side of running an evangelistic organization that specializes in witnessing, caring, sharing, giving, and meeting the needs of the churched and un-churched persons. Many people in the class began to financially support the team. The students learned so much from them.

Sometimes, while witnessing on the streets, students encountered opposition from people, but their experiences with the Faith-in-Action Team encouraged them to continue to lead people to Christ under many circumstances. Today, many of these young men and women are leaders, pastors, teachers, and community workers.

The Faith-in-Action Team invited a former Jehovah's

Witness to share information and strategies about how to witness to other Jehovah's Witnesses. The young man who talked with the class had been an administrator in the Jehovah's Witnesses movement. He explained that they were heavily indoctrinated with the Jehovah's Witnesses doctrine and, consequently, lacked liberty. He told us what happened when someone shared the liberating Gospel with him—it helped him to think, reflect, and take action to accept God's Word in his heart. As a result, he realized he could be free. Subsequently, when we evangelized on the streets of New Orleans, we used this information to shape our message.

Other Teachers

I can remember students bringing people from the streets to the Bible Study. Some of them continued to attend and grow with the group. The students learned from each other, from visitors who came to share their journey, from seminary professors, and from their personal journeys as they decided to follow Jesus. They also learned from doing—practicing what they had been taught. Young preachers learned from being invited to preach at churches in the community. Teachers learned by being asked to lead workshops, speak, and conduct retreats.

Sometimes the adult class struggled with some of the principles being discussed. I can remember the struggles of Donald Boutté. He would ask questions over and over again. Lisa would say, "That boy is hard to understand." We watched Donald grow over the years and study hard. He later became one of the Bible Study teachers. Today, he is Pastor Boutté. Lisa is a powerful teacher of the Word and an administrator in the public school system.

I believe one of the crucial teachings that was demonstrated more than it was verbalized is that we are all one in Christ. Women and men taught and were treated equally as children of God. Leaders in their own right, they learned that God is no respecter of persons. While I am not able to recall all of the lessons or names of persons who taught the Bible Study, a few that I can remember are: *The Abundant Life* by Ray Baughman and *Training for Service* by Orin Root. Several students helped to teach those series of lessons—Lisa Green Derry, Patricia Allen, Diane Smith, and others.

My husband, Felix, a deacon at our church, taught on the Miracles of Jesus; Rev. Douglas Taylor, now pastor of Bethel A.M.E. Church, taught Romans; Vanessa Polk, currently a Strategic Planning and Vision Development Consultant in North Carolina, taught Colossians; Rev. Ameal Jones, presently pastoring in Texas, taught Jude. The subject of lessons and the names of those who led the classes are numerous; and though not all are listed within these pages, the impact each teacher made on us was no less noteworthy.

Although both men and women were used to proclaim the Gospel, and despite the fact that our home was open to them as they studied the Word of God, some of the men who witnessed this and are pastors today do not permit me in their pulpit because I am a woman. I take it in stride, as I am reminded that they are still under construction. God blessed me to be instrumental in helping them develop their ministries. This is why I do not take credit for the ones who are successful and doing well, or blame for those who are still struggling. It's God who is working through the Holy Spirit in each of them.

Igniting Gifts
Developing Leadership

So Moses heeded the voice of his father-in-law and did all that he had said. And Moses chose able men out of all Israel, and made them heads over the people: rulers of thousands, rulers of hundreds, rulers of fifties, and rulers of tens. —Exodus 18:24–25

The Fire Becomes Portable

One day, the Holy Spirit touched me on the shoulder and said, "What will become of all of this learning? How will others benefit from what they have learned in this Bible Study?"

Before I could make any plans, the Holy Spirit provided opportunities through pastors and leaders in the community who heard about the Bible Study and began contacting us for help in developing various ministries in their churches. Their requests included help in building their Sunday Schools, presenting educational workshops, facilitating retreats, etc. Some asked for seminars to introduce people in the rural communities to the study of the Word of God.

These were just some of the opportunities that became available to the class. I didn't know if we were ready to meet any of these expectations. Because I held a Master's in Religious Education, I thought that I would have to do most of the work. However, when the opportunities were announced in class, students volunteered—they had a mind to work. Although they did not have letters behind their names, they brought experience, skills, and knowledge of organizing workshops, retreats, and seminars for large groups of people. I got an even better understanding of what Jethro said to Moses: "You have the needed leadership. Put some guidelines in place and the people will serve."

Isn't that just like the Holy Spirit? He is always ahead of us in helping us to do the will of God.

In our midst, there were the people who could

handle the assignments. Vanessa Polk was talented in visual arts and gifted in organizing and putting together educational packets (including paperback materials and Bible tracts) for different things that we were asked to do. There were others in that group who had skills in teaching, who had developed a love for sharing the Word of God with other people. So we began to accept invitations to train others, often volunteering to do this work. It was like an apprenticeship that the Holy Spirit had arranged.

Revival

One of the first opportunities we received to see the Bible Study leadership develop was when a local pastor asked for some preachers to conduct his revival. He needed preaching for three nights, so we sent three preachers: Fred Luter, Donald Boutté, and Charles Duplessis, each now pastoring churches of their own.

Retreats

The really big assignment that the Bible Study class received to prepare for a large group came after I went to sing one night at the First Baptist Church in rural

Vacherie, Louisiana. Rev. Lucien Garrett heard that I was in seminary and that we had a Bible Study at the house. His sister, Bernadine Garrett, approached me about having a Bible Study there, and stated that if we came on a Saturday, the local elementary school would be available.

Well, I brought the idea back to the group and they were excited! We had to travel down Airline Highway and catch the ferry across the river to Vacherie, which is about 60 miles upriver from New Orleans.

It was so exciting; it was beautiful. You could feel the group's enthusiasm about getting to conduct that retreat for the church. But, when we got to the elementary school that Saturday morning, very few people were there. Rev. Garrett got on the phone and started calling his church members. I could hear him talking, "Where's your mama? Wake her up! Didn't I tell y'all to be down here for eight o'clock? We got a workshop. Get up! Get the children up! Come, come so y'all can be a part of this retreat."

Many had not come because they didn't know what a retreat was. However, by the time he finished on the phone, there were about 100 people there. They broke down into smaller classes, and we were there for the whole day—until about 4 o'clock. It was rewarding for us, for the pastor, and his congregation. They told us how much the experience meant to them, and how they had not understood what a retreat was. Now, they knew.

Another rural church called us to conduct a Sunday School workshop, and it was another good experience. The students in the Bible Study kept their ears open and sought opportunities to use their skills. As the Bible Study class matured, I watched leadership develop among them. They began to take over. They knew what had to be done, and they knew how to do it. They knew how to set up trainings, and found themselves volunteering for different organizations. One of the primary organizations was the Faith-in-Action Team.

Witnessing

Working with the Faith-in-Action Team was an opportunity to train leaders in the area of witnessing. Students set up places to witness. They took to street corners, brought out speakers, and sang, preached, and testified. I remember one cold winter night, Marshall and Chip set up a place to witness and touch people's lives right on the neutral ground next to the Krauss Department Store on Canal Street.

There in the cold, in the dark, with just the streetlights, preaching, teaching, and witnessing took place. Students were taught how to witness. They were taught that they needed to go in pairs. They were taught that while one is talking, the other should be praying. They were taught that young men should approach young men and young women should approach young women, so that there would not be confusion about their motives. It would be safer and easier for them to talk to people with whom they had things in common, such as gender. Some of the students brought people whom they met on the streets to their churches so that they could accept Christ and become a part of a family, the body of Christ.

Reading

As the study progressed and leadership developed,

we began to focus on improving the literacy of the poor readers in the group. I attribute the fact that students were not ashamed to be helped, as they read aloud, to the personal impact small groups have on strengthening individuals. One of the young men who had difficulty reading now makes a six-figure salary and teaches Sunday School. Many of the students went back to school. Some returned to college and received their degrees. Some returned to vocational school and prepared themselves for life. Today, some of them are pastors, teachers, and leaders—actively working in churches as well as the community.

Effectiveness

Most of the preparation for leadership was developed by practicing what needed to be done. There were not a lot of academics taught, rather more leading by the Holy Spirit. We learned through trial and error. The students learned some things that they should do and some things they should not do. They learned that most of the things they were doing were right, and people were accepting Jesus. People were finding their way back to the family of

God and being baptized. When we went out witnessing with the Faith-in-Action Team, we went into barrooms and talked to people. In those places we found people who had grown up in a Christian environment, but had lost their way. They would say, "I know I need to be back in church. I know I need to get my life together. Thank you, and pray for me."

When we went into the public housing facilities, we heard young men and young women say, "Pray for us."

We learned to spot the leader of a group. They might be in a huddle gambling and sometimes dealing drugs. If we really, really observed, we could pick out the leader and begin to talk to him. He would get all of the others together.

Leadership was developed as students learned from each other. Remember, I said that there were not many home-based Bible studies or weekly Bible studies in the churches when we began. But, God always puts things in place that need to be there. He knew what this city needed and what these young students were seeking. He used this Bible Study as an instrument to get them where they needed to be.

Emerging Leadership

We began to see evidence of leadership development and training even though we didn't call it that; we didn't know it was that. We were just excited about fulfilling the invitations to lead and teach. It was a great period of preparation. What stood out most was that these young adults were committed to the Lord. They surrendered to Him, and they were committed to the Bible Study in the sense that they wanted to do what they felt God was leading them to do.

Leadership was an element that we did not recognize until years after the Bible Study had ended. As we look back, we see what God was doing all along. He was developing those whom He had called to lead. And even today, some of the former students will mention that they learned things during that time that they use now. Many methods and principles that they picked up as a result of being in the environment have made a difference in their ministries today. As John Maxwell's Leadership Bible says very clearly, "We are created in the image of God and God is a leader. If we are created in the image of God, we are leaders, but we need to be developed." That is what God was calling for in this home Bible Study—that students might learn how to lead and that they might develop skills that were already gifts within them.

The Female Factor

One dynamic regarding leadership that was pushed into the background was the fact that, as a woman, I started and led the group in which there were so many young men. They came and seemed not to have a problem. At that time, there was so much focus on young men that the Holy Spirit had to tug at me and say, "You're leaving out the women. You're leaving out the females."

As such, we began to also use the women in the group to be teachers and trainers. Lisa was one of the first teachers and did an excellent job. Vanessa also did an excellent job. My church had indoctrinated me to push male leadership, but I felt in my heart that something was missing. I did not even recognize that along with my husband, I had taken the role of leader in the Bible Study. We had no problem sharing the leadership, but I was the more vocal one. I am still very vocal today. I saw to it that those things that needed to be done were done and was the spokesman, or rather "spokeslady," for the Bible Study.

Whereas the focus had been on men in the past, the Lord helped switched my intense focus, and I became aware that I needed to also be an encourager of women. At that time, I had not accepted my call to the preaching ministry, but I did know that women needed to be encouraged and pushed forward to do what God had put on their hearts. So the atmosphere of the Bible Study began to change a little. In fact, some of the young men began to complain about me saying that I was "too pushy." They complained that I was "taking over" and not playing a "woman's role."

Even when I accepted the call to preach in 1986, before the Bible Study ended, some of the men had difficulty accepting my call to the preaching ministry.

Nevertheless, through all of that, they learned many things from me. The Holy Spirit put "stuff" in me that they needed to hear. They also learned from Felix. The Holy Spirit placed things on his heart that only the young men needed to hear and to see; likewise I was often used to encourage, support, advise, and counsel the young women. For many of them, Felix was a father image.

The preparation of female students to use their leadership ability became apparent. Women were liberated in this class. God used me to speak in many different churches to deliver His Word, especially for Women's Days, and women heard about the Bible Study. Some inquired about it and came, while others were discouraged from attending by their pastors as well as other people.

When women came to the study, they felt empowered to use their gifts and talents and take their place as leaders. One such woman was Mary, who is now our daughter. She heard me preach for a Women's Day on the New Hope Baptist Church's radio broadcast. Later,

I received a letter from her saying how she was seeking a closer walk with God. She knew Him already, but wanted to grow. Mary was a young adult from New Sarpy, Louisiana, and would drive down to New Orleans to attend Southern University at New Orleans.

Mary's car broke down after she started coming to the Bible Study, so she began to stay with us to go to school. Rev. Boutté jokingly says that Mary came to Bible Study one night and never left. She became a leader in her own right, loved the Word of God, and loved to teach it. Her interest was in adolescents—particularly adolescent girls. She became a member of Christian Unity Baptist Church and helped to lead the adolescent girls' ministry, called the Fruit of the Vine.

Today Mary is the founder of a nonprofit organization called AJAMM, an acronym for my name, Audrey Johnson, and Myrtle Magee, a pioneer pastor in New Orleans and the founder of The Way Jesus Christ Christian Church, before her death in 1987. AJAMM is an organization that ministers to women in ministry. We use the word "ministry" broadly, not just for preaching. Mary has been the leader of this group, and she's done a very good job. She is a deacon at Deliverance Community Baptist Church, where Rev. Troy Johnson, my son (who was also a student and then teacher at the Bible Study), is her pastor. Mary is his administrative assistant.

This has been an exciting journey, watching leaders develop and watching women become empowered to use what God has given them. There are women out there right now whom I see and you can see, on whom God has His hand. Yet, it is clear that they are afraid to step forth, primarily because of the traditions of men who are in leadership of our churches. So, our prayers continue to be with them, that they will find their place and become liberated—delivered from spiritual shackles and chains; that they may do the work that God has called them to do.

Continued Leadership

The Bible students were involved in many different ministries. Sometimes it was just individuals from the group providing leadership, sometimes it was the entire group, and sometimes it was several members of the group together. Whatever their skills were, God used them to make a difference in the church.

The leadership, as we see evidence of it, has developed tremendously. Some of the persons who were trained at the Bible Study and continue to use those skills as leaders include Rev. Fred Luter, pastor of Franklin Avenue Baptist Church; Rev. Charles Duplessis, pastor of Mount Nebo Bible Baptist Church; Rev. Charles Garrison, pastor of New Genesis Bible Church; Rev. James Wynne, pastor of New Orleans East Bible Church; Rev. Donald Boutté, pastor of St. John Missionary Baptist Church; Rev. Michael Polk, pastor of Trinity A.M.E. Zion Church in Wilson, North Carolina; Rev. Dr. Stephanie Nicholas Taylor, assistant pastor of Bethel A.M.E. Church, Rev. Connie James, an associate minister of Ebenezer Baptist Church, and many more.

We continued to develop leadership among women to enable them to stand firm and not feel threatened about speaking. Some of them are now teaching, preaching, and serving in other areas of ministry as leaders in the church. Some are recognized by their peers as ministers who are capable of effectively carrying out ministry with creative thinking and leadership skills. Some have found their way into other professions using the leadership skills they acquired through the Bible Study.

There are many who use their skills and knowledge from the Bible Study to move onward and empower other women to stop listening to discouraging voices around them and hear the voice of God as He calls them to do His work. Some of the women answering God's voice are: Elizabeth Luter, First Lady and leader/teacher of the Women's Ministry at Franklin Avenue Baptist Church; Beverly Wells Criddle, a leader in the Music Ministry at Franklin Avenue Baptist Church; Thriawer Duplessis, First Lady, leader of the Women's Ministry, and Worship Leader at Mount Nebo Bible Baptist Church; Lena A. Washington, Couples' Mentoring Ministry of Franklin Avenue Baptist Church; Karen Johnson Williams, a Minister of Music in Houston, Texas; and many others.

The Future Leaders: Our Children

As the Bible Study grew, young parents became concerned because their children were very busy and distracted their attention. We knew that we had to resolve this problem, so we began to use some of the teenagers as baby sitters. We had no Bible class for the teenagers or anyone who could teach them how to work with the children of different ages. At least, that's what we thought; but we were mistaken. Remember, the Lord had shown me that everything the church needed was in that room.

When the concern was voiced, Mrs. Bertha Johnson, who taught children in Sunday School and Vacation Bible School came forth and introduced us to a couple, the Petes, whose ministry was in the area of child evangelism. They were working in the community to reach children for the Lord. When they were approached, they volunteered to train those who were interested in working with children. In order to meet this need, a child evangelism class was scheduled an hour earlier than Bible Study—from 6:00 p.m. to 7:00 p.m. The child evangelism training lasted approximately six months.

During this time, Sister Bertha and Brother Pete encouraged Troy, our second son, who was 12 years of age at the time, and William and Joann Rogers, both 13 years old, to attend camp to become certified child evangelists. It was a two-week camp held in Dry Creek, Louisiana. The training included the use of visual aids and how to deal with group and individual behaviors. They conducted a series of outdoor Vacation Bible Schools throughout the Dry Creek Community. As a result of their training, we added several more Bible classes, and the house was filled with special sounds—babies crying, children running and singing, and in the adult classes, laughter and questions for the teachers. In the den were the classes for the toddlers and children. The teenagers were in the boys' bedroom. The babies were in our bedroom. The children's teachers alternated. The teachers were Sister Bertha, William, Joann, and Troy. Children accepted Christ in that room. Their parents would make arrangements for their baptism at their church. Members of the adult Bible

Study taught the teenagers, and later Troy began to teach teenagers. Different adults and teenagers cared for the babies. Today, both Troy and William are pastors, and Joann is an elementary school principal in Florida.

The Fire Still Burns

Reflections and Testimonies

Reverend Troy Johnson
Pastor
Deliverance Community Baptist Church
New Orleans, Louisiana

What About the Children?

My brothers and I grew up in a home that was open to the public. At any given time, there were people in our home. They were not necessarily blood kin, but were considered our extended family. We grew up with a host of uncles, aunts, brothers, and sisters who were not bound to us by blood. We were accustomed to having many people around. The home in which we lived had what we considered a revolving door that did not lock, so people came in at any given moment. With or without invitation, people poured in.

Our parents were mentors to many, old and young alike. As a result, we were used to sharing them with others. Therefore, when the Bible Study started, it did not feel like an invasion; it felt natural. I called the Bible Study an extension of the natural. But who ever would have imagined that the several on the dining room floor would grow to over 80 in the living room, dining room, den, and bedrooms!

People came from every walk of life and were not bound by denominational affiliation or cultural experience. The common tie was hunger; they were focused because they were hungry for spiritual food. Hungry for the Gospel, they came to the house early and left late, and they came just as they were—spiritually broken, bruised, and hurting. I discovered that hungry people would tell other hungry people where to find food, and that is just what they did, they told. We did not advertise. No billboard, no television spot, no gimmicks, or props, my parents just served what hungry souls needed, and that was the Word.

Sooner than later, many people came from work bringing their children with them. The children would come to the den to do homework and watch television. There was no plan put in place for them. It was almost as if they just appeared. I believe that this was not the result of poor planning but that my parents and we, "the boys" (as we were called), never imagined that it would grow this big and in such a short time. Actually, we boys had not a clue to what was happening but just allowed ourselves to go for an exciting ride that lasted 10 years.

Because the Bible Study had grown so large, with parents bringing their children, we found ourselves in what I consider a pleasant dilemma. More children appeared as the months and weeks rolled by. Not only did kids come as more people attended, but Bible Study students started getting married and having children! The numbers kept growing and growing. Before we knew it, the house was filled with children. The house on Fairmont was a symphony of noise—from the children, the adults, the teenagers, and the toddlers. The task was to get the symphony to play in key and all at the same time.

What about the children? No one from the Bible

Study rushed to teach the children because they did not want to miss the lesson being taught at that time. While the children were important, their parents' desire to be fed spiritually was greater. The children became a distraction because they were so busy. Discipline and Bible Study simply did not make a good couple.

After a period of time, I became the official baby sitter. I would watch the children in the den and try to keep them occupied while their parents were in class. Soon, there were too many kids for me to handle by myself. I was not equipped to work with the children. The problem went on for a period of time until concerns were voiced. The parents wanted something more than babysitting and homework. They wanted their children and teenagers to also be in Bible Study.

Mrs. Bertha Johnson, who was a student of the Bible Study and also a children's teacher, said that she knew of a couple who were child evangelists and would be willing to come to train and help. This couple, the Petes, came to the house one day to meet my parents and talk about how they could help. They agreed to train those that were interested in working with the children. Some students responded, but not many. Mrs. Bertha took on the responsibility, and later there was an opportunity for some of the teenagers to go away and also be trained as child evangelists. William Marshall, Joann Rogers, and I were asked to attend the training. At that time, William was 13 and Joann and I were only 12, but we were allowed to attend the two-week training in Dry Creek, Louisiana.

At the training we slept in cabins. We were taught how to use flannel boards, books, and other training materials, and we conducted a few Bible Study sessions in the surrounding Dry Creek area. It was an exciting time, but I do not believe we knew the magnitude of this responsibility.

We came back excited about what we had learned and we later assisted in teaching the children. As a result of this training, classes were added. The children and toddlers were in the den, the teenagers were in Felix and David's room, and the babies were in my parents' room.

These classes grew to full capacity. One of the reasons they grew so fast was because young people brought other young people and children brought other children. We taught and children and young people accepted Christ. Over time, the toddlers grew to be children and children grew to be youth. Some accepted Christ as their personal Savior. We encouraged those who accepted Christ to be baptized publicly at their local church, and they did.

Who could have known that the Bible Study would grow to such a magnitude? Who ever could have figured that God's plan was to reach, teach, and save families in this way? The ongoing effects of this home Bible Study would prepare young people for a lifetime. William Marshall is the pastor of evangelism for the Franklin Avenue Baptist Church. Joann Rogers is a school principal in Florida and I am the pastor of the Deliverance Community Baptist Church. Life is made up of moments, and from moment to moment, our lives are being molded, even though we may not know or recognize it.

Reverend Donald Boutté
Pastor
St. John Baptist Church
New Orleans, Louisiana

This is God's House

I became pastor of the St. John Baptist Church in New Orleans in May 2003, and I am very certain that I would not have made the journey to this junction in my life if it had not been for the love, long-suffering, patience, concern, and care that I received from the wonderful couple whose home I visited every Tuesday night for over 10 years.

It was the spring of 1977 when my friend, Willie Williams, came to me, excited about his new discovery. He had attended a worship service at the New Hope Baptist Church. During that service he met a group of young men who were, as he stated, "sold out for the Lord." He told me that he had given his life to Christ and was now a new creature determined to walk in the newness of life. He had come to me to get me to surrender my life to Christ. I could tell that he was excited and, though I was not really interested in all the religious jargon he was now spouting, I tried to appear attentive. We stood in the courtyard of the apartment complex from six in the evening until one the next morning. Finally, I could endure his excitement no longer and I sent him away frustrated that I did not surrender my life to Christ. I attended church and did not think that I needed anything else.

In the fall of that year, I moved, and Willie came by the new house still excited about his relationship with the Lord. Once again, he entreated me to really make Christ Lord of my life. Once again, he had made a new discovery. He had attended a Bible Study at a home on Fairmont Drive and he wanted to see if I would be interested in attending the next class. At first I hesitated, but then I agreed to attend the next Bible Study meeting. Tuesday came and Willie came by to drive me to the Bible Study. I tried to back out, but he could see through the lame excuses that I tried to give for not attending.

We arrived at this home, located in a quiet tailored community. We drove up the side driveway of the home and entered through the back door. Willie entered first and I followed. Then it happened. As soon as I crossed the seal of the door there was this amazing sensation. There was an unexplained peace and tranquility that radiated through this home. Later I discovered many of the other Bible students had experienced the same thing. Willie introduced me. "Audrey, this is Donald. I brought him tonight to see if we could save this sinner."

We all laughed and then she introduced herself, "Hi, Donald, I am Audrey Johnson. Welcome."

There was something about her smile and welcoming handshake. There was a genuine quality about it that made me really feel at ease and welcomed.

By this time, we were standing in the kitchen. Audrey said that the children had not finished dinner, but that the Bible Study would begin at seven. She asked if I wanted something to eat. I declined. Her three sons were seated at the table. They were playful and very happy. They greeted us and started to play and joke with us as if they had known us all of their lives.

When Audrey's husband entered the kitchen, she smiled and said, "Baby, this is Donald."

He did not pay attention at first; he was hurrying his youngest son out to football practice. Once again she said, "Baby, this is Donald."

This time he looked up. He said, "Hey, man, how are you? I am Felix Johnson."

Felix captured my attention. He seemed the epitome of fatherhood. In my mind's eye, he was what every Black boy dreams of when he pictures a father. Felix is a tall dark man, very stalwart, with a deep voice, yet he displayed a gentleness and caring demeanor as he said to he youngest son, "David, let's go, man. We're going to be late."

There was something in his voice that made you know he had a deep love for his children. Just before he and the boys left the house he said "Baby, we're going. I'll miss class tonight."

As he smiled, he leaned over and gently kissed his wife goodbye. As a boy from a broken home who never knew his father, and as a young man with a new family of his own, I was blown away by what I had just seen. At that moment I said to myself, What if I could be that kind of father to my son? Still, there was this presence, an atmosphere in this house that I had never felt before in my entire life.

Promptly at 7:00 p.m., we began Bible Study. Audrey was the teacher for the night. There were about 10 people present. I headed toward the den because I was certain the class would not be held in the living room. You see it was a beautifully decorated room with a white sofa. Certainly, you don't let a group of strangers come in and mess up your good furniture. Nevertheless, Audrey led us to the living room. Before we could get settled, the door-bell rang and more people came through the door. This time, it was the young and old coming in. The room was filled to capacity. The young people were seated on the floor of the living and dining rooms.

Audrey began the lesson in the Gospel of St. John. I was very uncomfortable because I did not know the first thing about the Bible. Yes, I had been in church; still, the Bible was strange to me. Audrey took us through the "I am's" of the text: "I am the Good Shepherd," "I am the Bread of Life," "I am the Living Water," etc. There was something in the way that she presented this information that stirred up something in me and made me want to learn more about the Bible. Class ended and she asked someone to phone Mrs. Hattie Johnson, a close friend of the family who had been diagnosed with a rare muscular disease. We formed a circle and everybody with a prayer request was given time to present their need.

By this time she was on the line, so the room said in unison "Hello, Miss Hattie." Then the prayer began. Audrey prayed. The presence got stronger. It permeated the room until you could almost reach out and touch it. Audrey continued to pray and she prayed as if God himself was standing right before her. I had heard folk pray before; my mother and grandmother were praying women, but there was something different that I just could not put my finger on. At the end of the prayer, there was an invitation to accept Christ and some of the students came forward. After the plan of salvation was explained and they had accepted Christ, they were asked to go to the church of their choice, explain to the pastor that they had accepted Christ, and make arrangements for baptism.

I left Bible Study that night with a lot on my mind. When we arrived at my house, Willie asked if I planned to attend class next week. Even though the class had a profound impact on me, I played it off and my response was, "Maybe. I'll see when the time comes."

All week long I grappled with Christ and what Christian life is really supposed to be like. The next Tuesday arrived and Willie phoned to offer me a ride. I accepted. That week the lesson was more exciting and, although I struggled with some of the information, I really began to understand what was presented. Thereafter, I attended the class each week. I drove myself.

Then, this family surprised me again. It was apparently vacation time for them. Audrey explained to the class that she and Felix were going out of town to a family reunion, but not to worry, class would go on as scheduled. After class that night Audrey pulled Lisa, another student eager to learn the Bible, and me aside. She explained that she and the family would be going to Chicago, and she wanted us to handle the preparation for the class the following week. She stated that Harold Ray, a student from the New Orleans Baptist Theological Seminary, would be coming to teach the class. She wanted us to open the house so that he could conduct the class. She reminded us not to forget to call Mrs. Hattie during prayer time. Audrey stated that she would leave the key to the house in the garage. She explained they would be gone for two weeks. I was apprehensive about the assignment. What if something happened or something was stolen? Who would be responsible?

Audrey smiled and said, "This is God's house. If something happens He will take care of it. You just let the people in. God will take care of the rest."

Lisa and I did as we were asked. The people came,

Harold taught, and the class was blessed. I was amazed at the trust that this family had in God. After all, they had not known me that long. Why would they trust me with the key to their home? What an amazing trust in the power of God to protect.

The Bible Study was held for over 10 years every Tuesday night, rain or shine, hot weather or cold, holidays, even on Mardi Gras. During the entire time, not one thing was ever taken from the home, though literally hundreds of strangers walked through the door. There were so many strangers because some of the students would meet people at bus stops, college campuses, in fast food restaurants, you name it, and invite them to the Bible Study. And, while they had access to the entire house because there was a study group in every room, nothing was ever taken. The composer Cecil Martin was right when he penned the words "God Will Take Care of You." My admiration for this family and their dedication to the work of the ministry of Christ increased. They returned and I could not wait to relinquish the responsibility.

Savior Like a Shepherd/Just Suppose

Even though I had been coming to the Bible Study regularly and had learned a great deal about the Scripture, I still wrestled with whether or not I could, or should, become as dedicated as this family. After all, I was young with a lot of ambition and the demands of the ministry were not part of my plan to achieve the American dream. I bought my first house at age 26—one year behind schedule—but I still felt that I was on my way and did not want the sensation of the Bible class to interrupt my 10-year plan. However, I was to gain a new perspective.

Audrey and Mrs. Hattie Johnson's daughter, Karen, also a student in the class, were scheduled to do a musical recital at a local Baptist church. They both have beautiful melodious voices, so I looked forward to the recital. Meanwhile, the week before the recital, Mrs. Hattie went home to be with the Lord. The question became, should the recital be cancelled. Karen asked that it not be cancelled, explaining that her mother would have wanted it to go on. There were several songs they sang individually and as duets. Near the end of the recital, Karen sang "Savior Like a Shepherd Lead Me." Her voice permeated the sanctuary and a spirit filled the room. Karen became overwhelmed, so full of emotion until she could no longer sing. I imagined this was a very difficult task, in light of the fact that she had just lost her mother. Then it happened. I saw the spirit of God come upon this young woman and she gained a new strength in our very presence. Then she began to sing with even greater resolve. At that moment, I understood better what the prophet Isaiah meant when he said "and His train filled the temple." There was a holy filling in the church that night that I shall never forget.

Following Karen's solo, Audrey sang a song that, for me, was the invitation to discipleship. The words of the song, "Just suppose, just suppose God searched through heaven and he could not find one man willing to be the supreme sacrifice that was needed to buy eternal life for you and me. Had it not been for a man called Jesus, our souls would be eternally lost."

The words of that song echoed within me the rest of the evening. I remember deciding, as I was leaving the church that night, that I would surrender my life to Christ and really pursue discipleship. I had accepted Christ at an early age, but I knew that night that I needed to be serious about becoming a disciple for Christ and learn more and more about Jesus.

"And I will give you pastors." —Jeremiah 3:15

After my surrender to Christ, the next thing that I faced was trying to determine how to really become a dedicated disciple for Him. Naturally, I went to my church excited about my surrender to the Lord. However, my excitement was quickly dampened. My pastor did not share my enthusiasm. In fact, my excitement was met with some skepticism. At that time, I could not understand his reaction, however, it later became evident to me why he reacted the way he did. Notwithstanding, I still attempted to pursue a relationship with him. But the more I inquired of him about the Scriptures, the more estranged we became. Still, I wanted a relationship with a pastor, someone who could help me with this longing to know more about Christ and the power of the resurrection.

I began to get frustrated in my pursuit. Then it happened! Audrey had gone on a trip, I cannot remember exactly where. When she returned, she said, "Donald, I have something that I think you will enjoy." It was an article on the crucifixion of Christ based on modern medical research. Then she said jokingly, "I know how bad your eyesight is, so I had it enlarged especially for you."

At that moment, the Holy Spirit revealed these words, "And I will give you pastors according to mine heart, which shall feed you with knowledge and understanding." The Spirit revealed to me that I had been looking at the wrong qualifications for a pastor. I thought a pastor had to be male, presiding over a local church, and connected to denominational associations within the city. But, true and faithful pastors are leaders whom God has anointed with wisdom and understanding and who can unselfishly impart that wisdom to the disciple of Christ.

As Priscilla did with Apollos, so did Rev. J (as we now lovingly call her) with me and countless other students within the Bible class. She became the pastor who listened attentively to young men and women seeking guidance and understanding to the challenges that life brought forth in a changing world. She knew the right questions to ask when these young people were grappling with self-realization. Just as Barnabas had been a blessing to the early church as the son of consolation, we had in this era of our lives the daughter of consolation. Young men who could not get an audience with their pastor when they were struggling with their call to ministry or the command of God to pursue pastoral ministry could get an audience with Pastor Johnson, who spent countless hours with them counseling them in the struggle. Many of them are now in vibrant ministries throughout our country.

Unfortunately, some who received this guidance and on whose ordination committee she sat, now do not believe women should serve as pastors of churches. Still, because of her love for Christ, she counsels them when they come (and they do come when they face the winds of adversity), supports them in their ministry, and encourages them when the pressure of ministry mounts.

The Apostle Paul said in I Corinthians 4:20, "For the kingdom of God is not in words, but in power." I have seen the power of God work through Rev. J. When AIDS was viewed as leprosy, I witnessed this pastor go to hospitals and deal with dying children and parents who bore the guilt of infecting a child with the virus. I have seen African-American politicians (male and female) caught up in the corruption of politics seek out this pastor who would reserve judgment in order to minister to the hurt and brokenness of young people entering the political arena. I have seen her board planes to go and minister to young people who had come through the Bible class but now lived away and found themselves in crisis. I have seen her pay the mortgage for a family in crisis, using her own mortgage payment to do it. She has demonstrated before us that a real pastor has the heart of the sheep ever present before her.

For me, this pastor has been responsible for my understanding the power of the resurrection; the power that God gives that helped preserve a marriage and raise two sons; the power to understand the responsibility of being a good steward of the blessings God had bestowed upon me; the power to understand the need for academic preparation. It was her love for knowledge and her determination to grow in grace that prompted me to return to the university setting. (I now have a degree in political science and public management and am certified as a broad-based community organizer). She taught me that the power of the resurrection of Christ should be manifested in every part of our lives as disciples of Christ.

"But grow in grace and in the knowledge of our Lord and Savior Jesus Christ." —2 Peter 3:18

Each Tuesday night I went to Bible Study. I became more active in my local church. I began to have a greater appreciation and understanding of sermons from the pulpit. I became active in the Sunday School at my local church. My prayer life became more fervent and I could now spend hours studying the Scriptures.

Audrey was intentional about the students of the Bible class getting hands-on experience in teaching and evangelizing. Many weekends the students were street witnessing, attending seminars at other churches or seminaries, or conducting workshops or Bible institutes for revivals. Our work in Vacherie, one of the river parish communities outside of New Orleans, was particularly helpful in our development. Rev. Lucien Garrett and his church were very hospitable to our young group of disciples and often arranged for some activity where we could provide leadership. It was during these times that some of the students got an opportunity to write Sunday School material, develop curriculum, and even write some church music.

For Audrey, leadership development and church growth were priorities. It was Audrey who introduced to us Dr. E. K. Bailey, pastor of Concord Baptist Church in Dallas, Texas. She went to his Institute on Church Growth and came back energized by what she had experienced. This was the first year Concord had held the Institute and she encouraged some of the Bible class members to attend the following year. The next year, a group of us went. The Institute was comprehensive in the information it provided on leadership, discipleship, and stewardship. The presenters were knowledgeable and engaging. That year, Dr. Bailey had a barbecue at his home, and he spent time with us as a group and encouraged us to continue the pursuit of church growth in our local churches. We left the Institute determined to be vehicles to encourage others from New Orleans to attend.

The God Who Neither Slumbers Nor Sleeps

To those who attended the Bible class, there was no doubt that Audrey was giving prayerful attention to the direction of the Bible Study and the growth and development of the students. However, I was also blessed by my relationship with Felix. Felix, who is a deacon in his church, had a love for pastors, especially those who were dedicated to the exposition of the Scriptures. It was Felix who introduced me to many preachers from around the country. Whenever some nationally known preacher would be in town—Dr. Gardner C. Taylor, Dr. Samuel Proctor, Dr. H. Beecher Hicks, Dr. Wyatt T. Walker, Dr. John Bryant, Dr. A. Louis Patterson, Dr. Johnny Ray Youngblood, to name a few—I could count on getting a call from Felix and we would find ourselves sitting in the audience listening to great preaching. Wherever permitted, he had his trusted tape recorder. When it was not permitted, we purchased the tapes so that we could listen to the sermons over and over again. (Later, the family gave him a camcorder for his birthday, so now he can see the sermons over and over again.)

Sometimes, for hours, he would talk to me about the awesomeness of the call of the preacher and the need to support pastors. He said that we should support those pastors with a vision and encourage the ones without a one. He could find some good in any preacher and he would often remind me that nobody is perfect so we should choose to look for the good inside of everybody.

I watched Felix care for his family. He would buy small gifts for his wife for no special occasion. For instance, leaving church one Sunday we stopped at a bakery and bought a small cake. The baker asked what is the occasion and Felix said just put, "To Baby," an affectionate name he calls his wife.

I watched Rev. J and Felix care for his elderly father, aunts, and any elderly member of the church who needed attention. I watched them work with recovering addicts. I watched them open their home to the homeless and newly released prisoners. I watched them attend sporting events with their sons and many of the young men in church who needed encouragement in their pursuit of sports. I watched them minister to families who lost children to tragedy and death. Sometimes they did not have to say a word, it was just the presence of friendship. I watched them deal with the financial pressures of leading a family during tough economic times. But most of all, I watched them deal with the physical trials of life.

In 1995, Felix was diagnosed with cancer. Radical

surgery was the only option available. There were complications during surgery that necessitated a hospitalization of several weeks; a great deal of this time was in intensive care. I watched his family, especially his wife, attend to the minutest detail of his care. His sons would come and kneel in prayer for their father. His oldest son would always end his visit by kissing his dad on the forehead.

I tried to be supportive, but there was also fear, anger, and disappointment. I had witnessed this man's dedication to the ministry of Christ, so I could not understand why God would permit this to happen to this family. After all, God was supposed to be a protector. I was angry with God because he permitted me to develop a relationship with this family, and now it appeared that he was going to cause pain and disappointment. I did not know if I could stand to lose a friend like this and so, within myself, I questioned whether or not God was as faithful as we were declaring or would he disappoint in the end.

Audrey always sensed when something was not right

with me. She pulled me aside and said to me, "Donald, it is times like these that you have to trust God, even when you don't understand it." Then she reminded me what Felix would say, "I am not sitting up all night worrying about my problems; I have given them to God. Since he neither slumbers nor sleeps, it does not make sense for both of us to stay up all night, so I'm going to bed."

Felix is very witty and has a great sense of humor, which he uses to the glory of God. Audrey reminded me of the trust that Felix had in the Lord. Well, needless to say, God gave him a complete recovery. Today, we still sit in audiences listening to great preaching.

When I shared with Audrey and Felix that I was being considered for pastor of St. John, they were as excited as I was. They encouraged me throughout the process. On the night that I was installed as pastor, I looked out in the audience and there was this wonderful couple whom the Lord used to make my journey possible. Oh yes, Felix had his camcorder and, even though he is not on the tape himself, I will always picture and remember the man behind the camera.

As I stand in the pulpit of St. John Baptist Church and look out into the congregation, I am very much aware that it was those years spent in the Fairmont Bible Study, along with being mentored by my own contemporary Priscilla and Apollos—Rev. Audrey and Felix Johnson—that helped prepare me for this pastorate. To date, I have been married for 32 years, my sons are now adults and living on their own, and I am entering a period of my life where I will be required to mentor and develop leaders for Christ. I know that I am standing on the shoulders of two great people who love the Lord with all their heart, soul, and might.

Lisa Green Derry
Sunday School Teacher
Christian Unity Baptist Church
New Orleans, Louisiana

And they overcame him by the blood of the Lamb and by the word of their testimony. —Revelation 12:11

Reflections About Tuesday Night Bible Study

When I was a child, I spoke like a child, I thought like a child, I reasoned like a child; when I became a man/ woman, I gave up childish ways. (1 Corinthians 13:11)

The above Scripture reflects the process that became an integral part in the origin and growth of the Tuesday Night Bible Study at 3825 Fairmont Drive. As a child growing up in the Methodist church, I did what children were expected to do once they reached "the age of accountability," as was taught by the church. At the age of 12, I was confirmed and baptized into the church. I did this as a child. I thought as I was programmed to think.

The act of accepting one of the tenets of the Methodist church by submitting to "sprinkling" as a means of baptism was a good thing. I became a baptized, confirmed member of the Methodist church—a Christian. My parents and other church family saw that I regularly participated in church activities such as Sunday School, Vacation Bible School, and other youth-oriented programs. I now recognize that all of this was the foundation for the person God has shaped and molded me into.

The groundwork was laid. I began what I now know to be the transition from childhood to adulthood. The transition from "a babe" in Christ who could only swallow milk to a mature Christian who desired "strong meat" began. Little did I know that my childhood desire to have what I thought of as a more upbeat, hand-clapping, foot-stomping, body-swaying church experience would materialize and include all the above and more.

Not only did I become a part of a Baptist church where I clapped my hands, swayed and stomped my feet in time with wonderful, rich, spirit-filled gospel music, but I began to seek a closer walk with God, and became active in the church. God designed more for me. His Spirit convicted and convinced me of my need for more.

I submitted to water baptism, full immersion in the church's pool, while six months pregnant with my first child. God, in his awesomeness not only allowed me to grow into motherhood, but placed in my heart a desire for spiritual growth—a desire to learn more about him through his Word. Attendance at Sunday School, Sunday evening Baptist Training Union and midweek Bible classes became a regular part of my life. I needed to hear, learn and understand "the Word." I hungered for God's Word.

The hunger almost became insatiable. I needed more than my church could provide. I needed an intimate, non-threatening environment that supported clear, palatable, applicable Bible Study. I needed a Tuesday night, 7:00 p.m.–until, at the kitchen table or on the floor in the living room, small group, family oriented, Holy Spirit filled and directed Bible Study.

God in his infinite wisdom urged me to ask my aunt, Audrey Johnson, the woman whose heart and mind he had already prepared, to begin a Bible Study. She agreed and the rest is history. It is a history that is integrally tied to need, desire, unction, obedience, and fruit of hard, but rewarding labor. It is a history of which I am forever grateful to God. It is a history that has positively affected my life and set the stage for the call God has placed on my life.

The rich history of the Tuesday night Bible Study at 3825 Fairmont Drive is indelibly written in the very fiber of my heart and mind. Without the study, lessons about the Bible, lessons on how to study, prepare and teach, lessons about loving those who in some estimations were unlovable, lessons about parenting, lessons about how to stand and be joyful in the midst of trials and temptations, and lessons about how to depend on God's omniscience, omnipresence and faithfulness would possibly have gone unlearned.

I am certain that the numerous Tuesday nights spent at Bible Study in the home of Felix, Jr., Audrey, Felix III, Troy, and David were ordained by God for such a time as this. I am certain that our lives—my husband's, my children's, my grandchildren's, and mine—are better because of what occurred during the years at the "Fairmont Drive Theological Seminary."

Reverend William Marshall, III
Pastor of Evangelism
Franklin Avenue Baptist Church
New Orleans, Louisiana

Dear Pastor Johnson:

I was about nine years old when I started attending weekly Bible Study at the house on Fairmont. I remember sitting on the floor of your living room that was partially cleared of furniture. I recall the line-up of Bible teachers: Charles Garrison, Ben Lang, Fred Luter—all pastors now—and many, many more. The lessons served as a spiritual soup that fed my soul. I also recall the loving, contagious atmosphere in your home. I felt safe, accepted, and loved.

Do you remember the money you supplied when I took a mission trip with Brother Pete? I was trained in neighborhood evangelism. The Bible Study at your home provided a foundation on which my life with Christ would flourish. The exact details of the house are faded in my mind, but the Bible Study lessons and the people are clear and seem untouched by time.

One of your Bible Study teachers, Fred Luter, is the senior pastor of Franklin Avenue Baptist Church with over 8,000 members. I am the full-time evangelism pastor there now, with a beautiful wife, Stephanie, and a 10-year-old daughter, Elaina. I have so much to thank you for. I thank you and Felix for sharing your home to further the Gospel. The house on Fairmont planted many spiritual seeds in the lives of people. The seeds are not dormant, but active and alive. A lot of pastors in New Orleans and its surrounding areas can trace their infancy in the ministry to a woman named Audrey, a man named Felix, and the house on Fairmont Drive. I have heard about your recent illness and I pray for healing and strength.

Lorraine P. Davis
Deacon
Faith Church
New Orleans, Louisiana

Dear Audrey,

Coming up from a Catholic background where the Bible was essentially taken away from us, I grew up hearing "it (the Bible) is too hard to understand, and if you try to understand it, you will literally lose your mind."

Well, my husband, who was a physician working at a major hospital, worked with a friend who suggested that he attend the home Bible Study at your house. He did, and this, in turn, brought about a greater understanding of the Bible, after which he soon accepted Jesus as Lord of his life. He started to change right before my very eyes, I knew something was different about him but I could not put my finger on what or why.

He invited me several times but I refused to attend, not knowing that it was God who was drawing me to the Johnsons' because we knew each other years before. What happened next was just amazing. I decided to go some three weeks later and, to my surprise, there you were with a group of other people.

I did not realize, but the lessons were getting into my very core. I knew I was dealing with something new to me. Not that I had never heard it before. I was attending church every Sunday. The Bible was being read to me, but it had never gotten in me as this new revelation. I bought a Bible and kept on attending. I knew of Jesus, but He was not Lord of my life. I was not saved and didn't know that. The Bible was easily explained to us, and I found out it wasn't just for the intellectual. Anyone could come to understand. There were different spokespersons every week, there was fellowship, there was victory in this life, and I loved everything about learning "this new thing."

I began by accepting the Lord and taking other Bible courses at other churches. I then realized I was in the wrong church to get where I needed to go. I came out of Catholicism and began to believe what I was hearing, "Faith comes by hearing, and hearing by the Word of God."

I got baptized. My husband got baptized, and we began to take my mother to your Bible Study, who by the way began noticing some changes in me. We began to evangelize the family. Since that time, all members of our house have been saved and most have been baptized. The rest is just history.

I sometimes think back on those days and can hardly believe how far we have come, all because of Bible Study at the Johnson's home. We established prayer partners there who taught us how to pray, how to walk by faith, and how good God is—how he just wants the best for his children, and mostly how to "walk the walk" and not just "talk the talk."

Some years later, we began to have Bible Study in our home, just like the one we first attended. It was work, and we were attacked at every turn. But, I can honestly say, it was all worth it, all because God can use somebody to save anybody. It has been a remarkable joy to walk with the Lord.

Jacqueline Osborne
Adult Sunday School Teacher
Green Forest Baptist Church
Atlanta, Georgia

In 1977, during the invitation at the end of one of the Bible studies, I acknowledged that I was not sure of my salvation. One of the young seminary students took me to a separate room and reviewed with me Romans 10:9–10. He asked if I had ever made this confession and assured me that if I had, I was saved and could not lose my salvation. I acknowledged that I had. He prayed with me and encouraged me to continue my study and growth in the Lord.

With that assurance of my salvation, Romans 10:9–10 became my favorite salvation Scripture. I also began to really study God's Word and seek his purpose in my life.

Some of the little things that have had a major impact on me are: 1) Audrey's comment that we should pray regularly for our pastor; that we should also pray for our pastor's wife; that her position is a calling in and of itself. These comments helped me to remember that my pastor is a man first, with a special calling on his life, but subject to temptations and failing like the rest of us. This also suggested that I should be open to opportunities to encourage my pastor with words, cards, letters, etc. 2) Audrey also encouraged us to highlight, make notes, and write in our Bibles. This may really seem like a simple thing, but I had always been taught as a child that this was something you dare not do! This was the beginning of my buying separate notebooks in order to take notes during worship service, revival, etc.

I have wonderful memories of seeing fellow attendees of the Tuesday night study announce their calls to the ministry, engagements (Fred and Elizabeth Luter), weddings, etc. It always amazed me how Felix and Audrey would allow the Bible Study to continue even when they were out of town or would not be home.

It was at the Bible Study that I remember Audrey introducing Becky and Charles Gilmer. They were right out of college and were seeking financial support of their ministry in Campus Crusade for Christ. They were not even married at the time. I became one of their supporters and have continued to this day. The Gilmers have six children and their oldest (Micah) is now planning his wedding. Can you believe it? I get monthly updates from them concerning their family, the ministry, etc.

Betty Rogers
Past Sunday School Superintendent
Christian Unity Baptist Church
New Orleans, Louisiana

I know that it had to be God who led Felix and Audrey Johnson to hold a weekly Bible Study in their home. There is no other explanation for a family allowing people—some of them perfect strangers—to pack their house week after week for years, whether they were home or not. This had to be God!

The Bible Study meant many things to me. It was a place where the Word of God was rightly divided and usually with practical application. So, it was stuff I could put to use in my life. It was a nurturing place—a place to grow in the Word. And we did grow.

It was a place of great fellowship. Lifelong friendships were formed. People felt a true kinship to one another. My husband and I still have friends that we met there. People in the fellowship were excited about the Word, we loved being there, and most people did not want to miss. We did not attend this fellowship/Bible Study out of duty as we sometimes did at church. People flocked there because they wanted to be there. People were hungry and eager for the Word.

I learned not only from the Bible lessons taught. I also learned from observing the Johnson family. From them, I learned what it meant to be consistent and faithful. I observed what it meant to be unselfish (I'm still working on this). We sang "Oh, How I Love Jesus" at the end of every meeting. I learned to want to love Jesus in the manner I observed love shown Him by this family. I learned what it meant to put Christ first!

My husband and I became stronger Christians during our time attending the Bible Study. Consequently, we became better servants in the local church. Many churches and ministries have greatly benefited from the Word that was taught and exemplified at the Johnsons' home.

How we praise God for you and your faithfulness!!

Joseph "Gunn" Rogers
Deacon
Christian Unity Baptist Church
New Orleans, Louisiana

Betty and I were new Christians and were eager to learn and fellowship. We wanted to learn from teachers and others. We wore out the furniture. I wanted to get to Bible Study early to lean up against the post.

I was not good or comfortable with impromptu things. When I was asked to lead the devotion, I responded with fear, but the Spirit gave me strength and courage. The Bible Study taught us to be courageous. We dared to be different. The experience strengthened us.

Elaine Williams Cavalier
Mentor for Engaged Couples
Franklin Avenue Baptist Church
New Orleans, Louisiana

Audrey and Felix,

So many times, we forget to say thank you to people who have helped us along the way. My path was dark, but I thought it was light until the prayers and the love of my sister Elizabeth, her husband Fred, and a family of people at 3825 Fairmont Drive began to call upon God for me over 23 years ago. He was a God whom I did not know, but later learned, through the teachings I received at the Fairmont Seminary, a God who knew me before I was born. Oh, what a blessing to my life.

Perhaps you are saying, "Well, that has been many years ago. Why are you saying thank you now?" Well, about two weeks ago, I was at a convention with someone who began to tell me about people who we once knew and how shattered their lives had become—how they were now back in darkness again. As they talked, in my spirit, I began to thank God for a good foundation—a foundation that has carried me over 22 years. It is a foundation in Jesus that if you all had not said "yes" to the call many years ago to open up your home to teach the living Word of God, I would still perhaps have been living in a dark world. My prayers are with you. I love you and thank you, thank you, thank you. Praise the Most High God for His love.

Love you.

Reverend Thomas Glover, Jr.
Pastor
New Covenant Baptist Church
New Orleans, Louisiana

Audrey Johnson's Bible Study was a Word Bible Study. The primary focus of the study was the teaching of the Word of God. People came to hear the teaching of the Word. The individuals who came to the study were hungry for the Word of God. In fact, they were hungry for God. Many in Jesus' day pressed in to hear the Word of God (Acts 17:11).

People stayed around the house for hours being saturated in the Word to get a better understanding. People sat on the floor to hear the Word, because the Word, not the seat, was important. Sometimes people sat on the ground and heard Jesus. Many young preachers and pastors had a forum to teach the Word. People received the Word gladly (Mark 12:37).

There was tremendous love in the Bible Study (1 John 3:14). The people in the Bible Study shared and helped people with personal needs. There was intercessory prayer for many people and God answered those prayers. Some people found their mates at the study.

We can allow the tradition of men to make the Word of God ineffective (Mark 7:13). The Bible Study was a break from tradition. Audrey and Felix gave their home and their hearts for the work of the ministry. They took a risk, because in those days, home Bible studies were not popular. I thank God for their obedience because many of us were blessed because of their faithfulness.

Reverend James Wynne
Pastor
New Orleans East Bible Fellowship Church
New Orleans, Louisiana

What Made This Bible Study Different?

The Fairmont Drive Theological Seminary was not the normal, traditional, ordinary Bible Study usually associated with home studies. This study was not sponsored or supported by an organization (Christian or secular) so as to promote a specific doctrine. It was strictly a place where the study was about and concerning the Bible. There was no attempt to convince anyone in attendance that he/she was going to hell or could not receive salvation because of some label (Baptist, Catholic, Methodist, etc.).

Since this was the approach, it was very easy for anyone to feel at home and a part of the Christian family. In every sense, the Bible Study was "Catholicism" at its best. Catholicism in the true sense that it was appealing to and included all people. Catholicism in the sense that it was able to break down barriers and present a universal appeal as was the original purpose of the "Great Commission"—to teach and make disciples of all mankind. Consequently, no one in attendance had reason to be ashamed to proclaim that he/she was a Methodist, Lutheran, Catholic, Pentecostal, Baptist, Full Gospel, or whatever.

With the feeling of being welcome, all were able to pay close attention to the instructions. Each instructor was aware that "the letter kills, but the Spirit gives life." It was a great manifestation of the grace of God. As a result, all in attendance could be certain of the following:

1. That God, not man, reserves the right to use persons with whom they agree or disagree. No one person knows it all! No one person has all knowledge or all wisdom.
2. Accepting others allows them to be whom and what God wants them to be, not what I want them to be.
3. Refusing to dictate and demand of others allows God to direct their lives. He is better than we are at such a task.
4. Attempting to embarrass another is counterproductive, debilitating, and can kill the last hope of self-respect.

5. I am not OK, you are not OK, but God is. God's grace is sufficient for me.

6. The more rules and regulations we make, the weaker we are spiritually.

What was the Impact?

1. Many who had lost hope became rejuvenated again.

2. Many who thought they had lost their salvation were reassured that they were only temporary prodigal, and returned.

3. Some who had given up on educational and vocational objectives began pursuit again.

4. The brokenhearted were able to look up again.

5. The spiritually blind received sight.

6. Prisoners—the mentally imprisoned—were able to remove shackles. Minds were renewed/transformed.

7. God's love was more evident than God's wrath.

Vanessa Polk
Vision Development Consultant
Vision by Design/Default Ministries
Roseboro, North Carolina

Impact of the Tuesday Night Bible Study

"And I will make you a great nation, and I will bless you, and make your name great; and so you shall be a blessing." Although they are the biological parents of sons, Felix and Audrey have given birth to a nation of sons and daughters whose numbers and influence extend worldwide. How could they have known that God's promise to Abram would manifest itself through them in such a profound way?

By faith, they opened their home, and I came to know the awesome wonders of having a personal relationship with Jesus Christ. As such, every experience I've had since leaving New Orleans 23 years ago has the fingerprints of the Bible Study on them. Audrey's holy boldness, the quiet and strong presence of Felix, and the quick-wittedness of Lil' Felix, Troy, and David are now ever-present attributes in my life and relationships with others.

In the small North Carolina town of Roseboro, the legacy of the Bible Study lives on through a Tuesday morning Bible Study in my home. On hardwood floors like the ones I sat on Indian-style, I disciple others just like I had once been discipled; and just as Audrey took me under her wings as an apprentice, I, too, invest in others and teach them what I have learned. The legacy lives on through every Sunday School and Bible Study lesson, every message "preached," every soul led to a saving knowledge of Jesus Christ, and every opportunity opened to me to equip the body of Christ.

The love of God and His Word were instilled in me and remain as my life's foundation. The resounding moral and spiritual values I was taught then still keep me in my pursuit of holiness today. I'm a woman living a changed life, not only because of the message I heard Audrey preach almost 30 years ago, but even more because of the life I see her living each day.

From the hardwood floors, to the kitchen table, to the ottoman in the den, from the foot of her bed, to standing in the hallway at the bathroom door, to riding in the back seat of her car, I received sound doctrine, Words of instruction, correction, and rebuke. I received love too strong to explain and too deep to measure.

These powerful and memorable experiences serve as blueprints for how I live, build relationships, and carry out my ministry today.

Karen Riley Simmons
Writer/Editor/Designer
Word for Word Publications
New Orleans, Louisiana

The Tuesday Night Bible Study gatherings on Fairmont Drive were a significant part of my life and spiritual growth as a young adult. When I reflect on those experiences, I readily identify at least two lasting benefits I received: a foundational recognition of the power, truth, and wisdom available in the Word of God and a family of Christian believers on whom I can rely for fellowship, encouragement, prayer, and godly counsel.

I was 19 when I began attending the Tuesday Night Bible Study, and though I had accepted Christ and grown up regularly attending church and Sunday School, I had not yet come to appreciate the fullness of truth, wisdom, and relevance of the Word in my life. Digging deep into the Scriptures and learning to incorporate them into my daily living was rewarding and exciting to me. I found myself searching the Bible for answers, reading it voraciously, and sharing the gems I found there with others in my Sunday School class and elsewhere. The Bible Study helped me to mature spiritually and was instrumental in my developing a lifelong habit of study and application.

Since the study's last gathering in 1986, I have resided in two states on separate coasts, only recently returning to live in New Orleans. Since my departure 17 years ago, many of the young preachers, teachers, evangelists and students who sat crowded side-by-side on the floor with me now populate the churches, pulpits, deacon boards, teaching posts, counseling seats, and evangelist circuits of our city and beyond. So many from the former Tuesday Night throng are still present, active, leading, and thriving in the Kingdom of God. The benediction repeated at the close of every Tuesday gathering thanked our Lord for all that he had done for us, all he was doing for us at that moment, and all he would do for us "one day." I rejoice to be able to witness those "one day" blessings he is so richly bestowing on Tuesday Night study alumni today.

As I settle into our city and again encounter former fellow Tuesday-nighters, the familiarity of their faces and the memory of the fervor and fellowship we shared give my homecoming a special dimension—these are individuals with whom and for whom I prayed and who prayed for me every week for years. The lasting effects of our mutual *agape* and long-ago *koinonia* helped sustain me during my years away and are welcoming now as I reorder my life again in New Orleans. Many remain close and are part of my New Orleans "family." The apostle Paul instructs us to continue loving each other as brothers and sisters, encouraging and spurring one another toward "love and good deeds" (Hebrews 13:1 and 10:24–25). Those of the Tuesday Night Bible Study have done that for me and I am grateful.

Mary E. Washington
Deacon
Deliverance Community Baptist Church
New Orleans, Louisiana

I was exposed to diversity at an early age. My family and I were members of a traditional Black Baptist church in my hometown of New Sarpy, Louisiana. On occasion, we were made to attend a "Spiritual Church," pastored by my mother's Nanan, Mother Carrie Jones. My heart and ear were attuned to the uniqueness of a woman as pastor and in leadership early in life.

Each Sunday morning before going to church, we would listen to the radio broadcast of the New Hope Baptist Church and upon returning home, we listened to the broadcast of the Gloryland Mount Gillion Baptist Church. I was mesmerized and my spirit captivated by the voice of the "preacher" and radio announcer by the name of Audrey Jackson Johnson. It was then that our spirits connected. I knew that I had to meet that great woman of God.

The first thing that I did was to find her address and

write her a letter. In the letter, I expressed how God had used her to minister to me in such a powerful and awesome way. I was a teenager at the time.

A few years later, I enrolled in SUNO (Southern University at New Orleans) and became friends with Saundra Frazier, Karen Johnson, and Ronald Mattere. Karen and Ronald were the founding directors of the Gospel Choralettes Community Choir, of which I became a member. The three, Saundra, Karen, and Ronald were instrumental in me coming face-to-face with the Johnson family. Karen invited me to attend the Tuesday night Bible Study in the Johnsons' home. I was searching and eager to learn God's Word and continued to attend the Bible Study. The Johnsons' home became and continues to be my place of refuge. Rev. Donald Boutté says that I came to Bible Study and never left. It blows my mind when I think of how God ordained and arranged all of the meetings necessary for me to become connected with the Johnson family.

You see, I was a small town girl, naive and ignorant

about what happens in a "big city." I could have been easy prey for the wrong hands. God planted me in the lives of people who were committed and called to making disciples.

When I look and reflect on my life, the words of Helen Baylor's song, "Our God is an awesome God; He reigns from heaven above with wisdom power and love. Our God is an awesome God," captures what I believe the power of God did to connect me to this family. It was his orchestration, direction, and mandate that led me to this family.

I was born the 13th of 13 children to Lovely and Clarence Washington, who were very nurturing, loving, and protective parents. As the 13th, I was not the result of practice. I like to think that they were bent on finally getting it right. Through wisdom and experience, they had mastered Parenting 101. They provided a spiritual base that connected me to my extended family that consists of Felix, Audrey, Lil' Felix, Troy, David, Ernest, William, Emelda, and more. This relationship has been a solace and protection for me from the hand of the enemy. God led me to a family that continued to provide the love, nurturing, spiritual growth and development that I need to make it as a woman on this journey we call life.

The Bible class, led by many great scholars, was where I became familiar with and committed to the Savior, Jesus Christ, who I had met as a child. This family challenged and continues to challenge me to live and stretch to become what I am destined to be. Felix and Audrey teach me daily what it means to love unconditionally. Many of you will never know the personal sacrifices that this family made to do ministry during the Bible Study days and continue to make as they are both maturing spiritually and physically. Felix and Audrey exemplify what the real meaning of ministry is. Their lives have been an open book that many of us have read from and learned so much about what it really means to be Christ-like.

As I travel around this city and country with Audrey, I hear repeatedly in mega as well as small churches how Felix and Audrey helped shaped and continue to influence the lives of many people. God has gifted and ordained this modern day priest and prophet to bring us into the kingdom for such a time as this. Words cannot explain what this family means to me on this pilgrimage through life from earth to glory.

Willie Williams
Graduate Student in Criminal Justice
New Orleans, Louisiana

My father and mother raised my three sisters, my brother, and me to attend church service and Sunday School every Sunday. It was not an option. On Sunday you wore your best clothes and marched to the sanctuary.

My childhood pastor, Minister Willie Williams, was blind. Yet it seemed he could see and hear everything as he strolled the aisle stopping by each Sunday School class to listen to the lesson being taught. He organized Morning Star Missionary Baptist Church with eight members on Tuesday, June 6, 1943. Ironically, I don't remember his funeral, for it seems as though he just disappeared to heaven.

I remember that going to church was an emotional and sometimes frightening experience. The screams and shouting, ushers running with fans to calm those kicking and throwing their arms about were regular occurrences. It was so common that I tried to sit next to someone I thought would not shout! Imagine walking slowly gazing at each pew to discern who's a shouter. After church we would say Sister Mary got the Spirit today, or the Spirit was high at church today.

The language or phrases used to describe, identify, or reference the church and the Spirit is quite different in 2004 compared to when I was younger. As a matter of fact, many would say that the entire genre or ideas of worship have taken on a whole new meaning and appearance. I remember two statements when I was younger that had a profound affect on me. After a revival one night, brother Setly Bridges asked me if I was sure that I was born again. I replied, "I go to church every Sunday. I even sing in the choir." His continued questioning led to my scriptural understanding of salvation. The second was Minister Audrey Johnson's statement, "Willie, we don't go to church, the church gathers together to worship God." She further stated that we have a tendency to live the way we think. "For example, if I believe that because I go to church I have no need to live righteously except on Sunday, I absolve myself from any real responsibility. However, if I understand that I am the church and Christ lives in me, then I have a daily responsibility to live for Him, not just on Sunday."

One day, Audrey informed me that she was going to start a Bible Study at their home on Fairmont Drive. She invited me to attend. This was a new experience for me because studying the Scripture was not always something I practiced. When I arrived on a Tuesday night, it was only about six to eight people present. We sat on the floor in a circle to study the Bible. We continued to meet once a week. I remember the criticism from the pastors, and even my father, who years later thanked her for her contributions that impacted the lives of many individuals. There were many critics who felt as my father did, that Audrey's motives were to circumvent local congregations. Those of us who attended knew that it served as an enhancement to the body of Christ.

Well, despite the negative press, the Bible Study grew and grew until people were standing in the hallway, kitchen, sitting in the bathroom and on the steps. They came from every church and denomination. There was a hunger and thirst for the taught Word. There was a void in the midst of church tradition. We were exposed to the best teachers and theologians. Felix Johnson, Audrey's husband, fed us the best home-cooked meals. My friend, Pastor Donald Boutté, always reminds me that the traditional churches we attended had a place and purpose in the community and, for the most part, served it well.

Technological advances and commercialism have ushered Christian television to new levels. Despite the fact that it has reached millions who might not otherwise have received the Gospel, it was the home Bible Study that most closely knitted together the human fabric of love and the spirit of Christianity exemplified by the early church in the Book of Acts, chapter 4:32–35. Thank you, Felix and Audrey, for helping me experience heaven on earth through your love and sacrifices.

Elizabeth Luter
First Lady of Franklin Avenue Baptist Church
Women's Ministry Leader/Teacher
New Orleans, Louisiana

Faithful at Fairmont

Ignorant of the full scope of God, blinded by traditional things, I was made whole.

Sitting on the floor at Fairmont Drive, I never dreamed that it would be the basis of a solid foundation. How would this be different from other cult-like home settings I'd previously experienced? Having been escorted personally out of others, literally by the hand of God, this one seemed promising. My spirit man would rest upon entering the doors. Why would I have been handpicked and chosen by God to be nurtured in such a way? Although I was only 21 at the time I entered the home for the first time, I was saved at 10 years old. However, I was committed to the life and work of Christ only two years prior to attending the home Bible Study.

Traveling all over the country and discovering new arenas, I'm amazed that the training I received has given me confidence to stand in the presence of many. All of the information I received protected me from following the new doctrinal cults that developed in my early 20s. The Word was my shield against "the everybody's doing it" clan. I developed spiritual muscle to fight against false doctrine that tried to envelope me. We were taught to draw our own conclusions, in spite of how confident we were of those who instructed us. We were trained to follow the hand of Christ only, so that the opinions and changes of others could never lead us off of God's ordained track.

Today, I continue to chase after the truth of God, having been well prepared to know the difference between truth and error.

The Bible Study never became our resting place, only our launching pad. We were never instructed to follow or worship any man or woman in authority there. Jesus Christ was high and lifted up along with sound doctrine. We were told that if the Word was new, then it wasn't true; and if it was true, it wasn't new.

Watching many run before me die, stumble, and fall, I attribute my steady pace to the grace of God and the Fairmont Foundation. I took my training there literally. I believed God's Word because of the manner in which it was presented.

Today, I cling to no man's traditions or doctrines because I was instructed to individualize and internalize the Christ of the Bible.

I give God all the glory for Felix and Audrey Johnson, their children, and their home. There are many independent Christians today, walking on the narrow road, beckoning others to come to the light of Christ because of the Christ demonstrated in their dwelling.

Edward and Lena A. Washington
Couples Mentors
Franklin Avenue Baptist Church
New Orleans, Louisiana

Dear Felix and Audrey,

To God be the glory for all the things He has done through you. We thank God for every remembrance of you and your obedience and commitment to your calling to open your home to so many. We came to your Tuesday night Bible Study through our friends, Michael and Vanessa Williams Polk; and the impact those studies have had on our lives can never be shared in the space allotted. However, we will share some of God's blessings:

• The blessing of knowing Jesus and the power of His resurrection;

• The blessing of sound doctrine that equipped us to be leaders and to stand up for the cause of Christ;

• The blessing of sincere spiritual nurturing from two individuals who loved the Lord and were committed to change the way Bible Study was taught.

When we first attended the Bible Study in 1978, we

both felt out of place. Everyone seemed to know so much more that we did about the Bible. We thought we could never measure up, so we were quiet most of the time. Little did we know that God had a plan, and we were in it.

Because of the spiritual foundation that was laid at 3825 Fairmont Drive; and because you never ceased to pray for us—"that we be filled with the knowledge of His will in all spiritual wisdom and understanding, walking in a manner worthy of the Lord; pleasing Him in all respects, bearing fruit in every good and increasing in the knowledge of God."

Felix and Audrey, because of who you are in Christ, we were able to become spiritual leaders of our family and church. We thank God so very much for your Christian example; and we pray that God will continue to strengthen your for even greater works.

We thank you again for blessing us with your gift of giving.

Reverend Fred Luter
Pastor
Franklin Avenue Baptist Church
New Orleans, Louisiana

A True Picture of the Early Church

As a babe in Christ, I had never been to a Bible Study. Even though I was "dragged" to church by my mom, our home church did not have an organized weekly Bible Study. My then-future wife, Elizabeth, invited me to a home Bible Study on Fairmont Drive in the Gentilly area of New Orleans. It was there that I met a family and a group of believers that would impact my life for years to come.

The Johnson family (Felix Jr., Audrey, Felix III, Troy, and David) opened their home every Tuesday night to total strangers. I have no doubt that there were many weeks when they wanted some quiet downtime, however none of us could ever tell it when we crossed their door seal. The Johnsons were the most gracious, most hospitable, most unselfish, and the most Christ-like family I had ever met. No matter how early we showed up on Tuesday night, or how late we stayed, they *never* complained—at least while we were there.

This home Bible Study transformed the lives of countless people over the years. Sharing seats on the sofa, sitting on the floor, and sometimes standing around the wall, we were hungry for spiritual nourishment; and my Lord were we fed! Pastors, ministers, seminary students, as well as many other believers taught us the Word of God each week. This home Bible Study was a true picture of the early church in Acts, chapter two. Worship, discipleship, evangelism, ministry, and fellowship were evident among these believers on Fairmont Drive. In fact, the spiritual growth witnessed in many churches across the city of New Orleans has often been influenced by believers who were "trained" at this life-changing Bible Study. My personal spiritual growth was ignited, fanned, and sustained each and every Tuesday night at what many of us have nicknamed "Fairmont Theological Seminary."

I am now pastor of the Franklin Avenue Baptist Church, one of the largest ministries in our city. God has blessed me to preach at seminaries, conferences, and seminars all over this country. No matter where I go, or will ever be invited, I thank God that I got my start on the living room floor of "Fairmont Theological Seminary"—a true picture of the early church.

Conclusion

The work of the Holy Spirit was evidenced in the growth and progress of the Bible Study. Many have testified about the impact of the Bible Study on their ministries and lives today. The 10 years that this Bible Study lasted created an environment of trust and family. The greatest joy was to be able to hear God's voice and see Him work on behalf of the entire group. This has been a recalling of what God will do when we follow as He leads. He led, we followed; so God gets the glory. We—Felix and I—realize that we were the conduit that He used to call people out of darkness into light; to restore those who were out of fellowship; and to train people as leaders.

It was important for Felix and me to continue to seek God's will for the next phase of our lives and this Bible Study. During the life of the study, we were seeking another church for fellowship. God sent Rev. Kirk Jones, at that time the pastor of Beacon Light Baptist Church, to visit the Bible Study one Tuesday night. Felix had been visiting Beacon Light occasionally, and he made the decision that we needed to consider this church as our new church family. We did join, and our attention began to focus on ministry at Beacon Light. We became involved in the ministry of that young church. I was appointed as minister of Christian education and Felix became a trustee and later a deacon. The Bible Study was still in progress. However, as I began to work with the members at Beacon Light and have workshops and seminars, we invited the Fairmont Drive students to many of the sessions and used some of them as facilitators for the sessions.

The attendance on Tuesday night at Fairmont Drive began to decrease and that was a sign to us that the work was done. Felix and I agreed that the Lord was saying, "It is over. You have completed this assignment."

We released the Fairmont Drive Bible Study in 1987. The joy is to know that we were faithful to our call.

May the Work We've Done Speak for Us.

www.ingramcontent.com/pod-product-compliance
Lightning Source LLC
LaVergne TN
LVHW090949080826
845145LV00003B/949

* 9 7 8 1 8 9 1 7 7 3 5 3 2 *